Study Guide to

Four Quartets:

Burnt Norton, East Coker, The Dry Salvages, Little Gidding

by T. S. Eliot

by Ray Moore

The Photograph of Thomas Stearns Eliot in 1934 was taken by Lady Ottoline Morrell (died 1938). (Public domain. Source: Wikimedia Commons.)

Acknowledgments:

The text of "Four Quartets" will remain copyright in the U.S.A. until 2039 and therefore cannot be reproduced in this book. However, it is readily available in printed form and on the Internet.

I am indebted to the work of numerous editors and critics. Once again, I stand on the shoulders of giants. Any failure to reference a source is an omission that I will immediately correct if drawn to my attention.

I believe that all quotations used in the book are either out of copyright and/or fall under the definition of 'fair use.' Once again, if I am in error on any quotation, I will immediately make the necessary correction if drawn to my attention.

My text is written in American English, but many of the quotations were written in Standard English. The main difference is in the spelling of some words.

Thanks are due to my wife, Barbara, for reading the manuscript, offering valuable suggestions, and putting the text into the correct formats for publication. Any errors which remain are my own.

Contents

Preface

My first encounter with Thomas Stearns Eliot (1888-1965) occurred in a classroom in Nottingham, UK, in the autumn of 1966. It was the start of my Advanced Level English Literature course, and our teacher, Mr. Dutton, brought in a record player and proceeded to play a reading of "The Love Song of J. Alfred Prufrock." As the words floated around the room, the twenty or so boys, having failed to find any sense in them, began to look confused and then frustrated. Most of us tuned out and just sat through it. I forget why Mr. Dutton played us that poem. Eliot was not on our syllabus, and our teacher certainly did not explain what "The Love Song" meant.

That memory, however, stayed with me, so that when on my Modern Poetry Reading List at Sussex University in the summer of 1970, I saw the name T. S. Eliot, I had certain expectations. I knew by that time that this was the man who had single-handedly transformed poetry from a popular form accessible to a wide audience into an esoteric sub-genre catering to a tiny coterie of intellectuals and academics. Against this initial prejudice stood only the haunting memory of those opening lines:

> Let us go then, you and I,
> When the evening is spread out against the sky
> Like a patient etherized upon a table...

How was it that I had remembered them from a single hearing four years before?

To my surprise, I found much of Eliot's poetry less 'difficult' than I had anticipated. That is not to say that I understood it all, but it was clear that he was writing about feelings and ideas that were familiar to me. Even the notoriously obscure *The Waste Land* had sections that were transparently clear. And then there were the words and the rhythms created by the words. Even when I did not understand them, they somehow demanded to be read aloud. I loved to roll them round in my mouth, savoring the experience.

My mind must have been pretty exhausted by the time I got around to *Four Quartets* because I found it difficult to make any sense of them. I ran out of time to consult the critics my tutor had recommended before the seminar on Eliot. Of course, there were still those parts that spoke directly and clearly to my own experience, as when I read:

> So here I am, in the middle way, having had twenty years-
> Twenty years largely wasted, the years of *l'entre deux*
> *guerres*-
> Trying to use words, and every attempt
> Is a wholly new start, and a different kind of failure...

I certainly was not middle-aged (though sometimes I felt like I was, and I certainly knew a lot about wasting time), but those words described precisely the struggle I had every time I sat down to write an essay and suffered a new kind of failure. And still, there were the words and their rhythms. I remember once playing a recording of Sir Alec Guinness (1914-2000) reading *Four Quartets* and just giving myself over to the music of his voice.

In thirty-eight years teaching literature, T. S. Eliot never appeared on the syllabus, though plenty of other notoriously 'difficult' writers did (Pinter, Plath, Auden, etc.). Every so often, I would pick up my *Collected Poems and Plays* and renew my acquaintance with those texts as one occasionally looks up a long-forgotten old friend. I would even venture into *Four Quartets*, though they still baffled my mind even as they delighted my senses. When I began producing study guides, I think I did a pretty good job on *Prufrock and Other Observations* (1917), *Poems* (1920), and *The Waste Land* (1922). However, when I decided to tackle *Four Quartets*, I hit a wall. Only recently was I drawn back to this text, and the present volume is the result.

Eliot's *Four Quartets* are normally published without line numbers. To aid the reader, quotations are listed by line number, starting with the first line of that particular quartet. The numbering is my own. A slight difficulty is encountered when the text has half lines. Nevertheless, since this guide breaks the poem down into relatively short sections, readers should have little trouble locating quotations.

Reading the Poetry of Thomas Stearns Eliot

I worry when someone says they really love a poem even though they do not understand it. Unless a reader is satisfied to sit back with the mind disengaged and simply allow the word-music of poetry to wash over them, some understanding of the ideas embodied in the text is essential to appreciating poetry. Sometimes, I am told that poems are open to individual interpretation, as though one interpretation is as valid as another so long as each is held sincerely. That is patently not true. After publication, a poem like any other text may no longer be the sole property of the author, but that does not mean that it becomes entirely mine just because I bought a copy and read it.

Interpretation must be firmly rooted in the text, and our reading of poetry should aim to understand fully the meaning of the words as they appear on the page. The poet's intended meaning is ultimately not our concern because what an artist consciously intends a work of art to represent or mean does not define or limit what it actually does represent or mean. Most of the time, readers have no clue about an author's intentions, and to claim to know the unknowable is to commit the Intentional Fallacy. On those few occasions when an artist has explained his intention in a particular work, this explanation is interesting but in no way definitive.

The interpretation of T. S. Eliot's poetry represents a particular challenge since some (though by no means all) of his poems are complex, obscure, and/or deliberately ambiguous. There are several reasons for this. First, Eliot was a classically educated scholar, and almost all of his readers today are not. His knowledge of Greek and Latin texts and the great writers of the European tradition was combined with wide reading in anthropology, philosophy, and Eastern mysticism. Second, Eliot deliberately appropriated for his poetry ideas and quotations from other writers, generally without acknowledgment. Scholars might have the time and expertise necessary to locate and explain such borrowings, but most of the rest of us do not. Third, Eliot was a Modernist in poetry. In reacting against the popularity of poetry from the Romantics through the Victorians to the Georgians, modernist poets came to see obscurity as some sort of guarantee that one was producing poetry. Eliot himself wrote, "Poets in our civilisation must be difficult. Our civilisation comprehends great variety and complexity, and this variety and complexity, playing upon a refined sensibility, most produce various and complex results. The poet must become more and more comprehensive, more allusive, more indirect, in order to force, to dislocate, if necessary, language into his meaning" ("The Metaphysical Poets," 1921).

On the issue of quotations, allusions and flat-out thefts in Eliot's poetry, Nasrullah Mambrol offers the following reassurance:

> In approaching Eliot's […] poetry, up to and including a poem
> as late as "Ash-Wednesday," which had been published in

1930, a mere five years before Eliot composed "Burnt Norton," a reader not armed with a cogent survey of the various sources that Eliot had called on for his network of allusions would likely feel unprepared for engaging the poetry [...] The case is quite the opposite with the poetry of the *Four Quartets*. It has its fair share of historical, literary, and biographical reference points, to be sure, but the separation between the poetry and the poet's sources, whenever he brings them to bear, is so narrow that it is doubtful that gaining or missing the allusion will contribute in any serious way to gaining or missing the meaning. ("Analysis of T. S. Eliot's Four Quartets")

Though each example must be judged on its merits, this seems to be a reasonable and reassuring point.

Nevertheless, the *Four Quartets* have a well-deserved reputation for being exceptionally opaque. Unlike the earlier poems, the reader is challenged not by the disjointed poetic form, which results from the poet's refusal to put in connectives, but the difficulty of the ideas. Eliot, we remember, began as a philosophy student writing his Ph.D. thesis (completed but never defended) on the idealist metaphysics of F. H. Bradley (1846-1924), which he found appealing due to its affinities with Indian philosophical sensibilities. *Four Quartets* sometimes reads like a philosophical treatise in verse. This is a work of Christian mysticism and mystical experiences, by definition, are impossible to explain fully in words or to comprehend fully with reason alone.

Matthiessen writes:

The reader of the quartets finds a sufficiently straightforward logic, but is confronted with realms of discourse largely unfamiliar in a secular age. Sustained knowledge of the dark night of the soul is a rare phase of mystical experience in any age [...], but it should not be forgotten that authentic poetry often takes us into experiences equally remote from our ordinary hours [...] (*T. S. Eliot*, 193)

G. Douglas Atkins seeks both to explain and justify the challenges this text:

Four Quartets is inexhaustible. No one can master it, and no one should try. I sometimes think that Eliot – at pranks, perhaps – sought to frustrate the reader, to employ the poetics of difficulty and adversity, to make his essay poem too strange for misunderstanding. (*Reading T. S. Eliot*, 2)

I have read many attempts to explicate these four poems but have usually been disappointed. Some critics claim that their meaning cannot be explained: the meaning is in the poetry and in the experience of reading the poetry. Thus, Dwight Longnecker writes:

The symbolists strove to use ambiguous or bewildering images

4

and language to bring the reader to the edge of a new experience of the numinous. Eliot is a master of this technique. He intends the bewildering, abstract, or obtuse images and language to break our literalistic search for merely denotative meanings. The strange language and imagery is meant to disconcert us and thus bring us to the threshold of a wider reality beyond the mundane and quotidian. ("Listening to 'Burnt Norton'")

Other critics make an effort to explain the poetic meaning in prose, but to me, their language is often just as challenging as Eliot's poetry while having none of the music of that poetry, so as a reader, I am no further forward. This explains why, contrary to my usual practice, I have quoted relatively little from critics and interpreters in this guide.

I recall a story (perhaps apocryphal) concerning another monumentally opaque work of the Modernist period, *Finnegan's Wake* (1939) by James Joyce (1882-1941). Joyce sent an early draft of a few pages to a friend together with copious notes explaining every pun and allusion. The friend wrote back to say that, without the notes, it would take someone a lifetime to read the book. Joyce replied that his readers *had* a lifetime! Some academics do devote, if not their entire lives, years to the study of texts such as *Finnegan's Wake*, but the general reader ignores these same texts. Personally, I did once wade through *A Shorter Finnegans Wake* as edited by Anthony Burgess but was no wiser at the end than I had been at the beginning.

This guide to Eliot's *Four Quartets* is not written for scholars who have the educational background, time, resources, and intellectual capacity to trace all of Eliot's sources, influences, and borrowings. It is for readers and students who want to read and appreciate Eliot's last great work. I certainly do not pretend to understand everything in these four poems, but at least I am honest about it!

I aim to offer a structure that will enable readers to understand, on the basis of the text, what Eliot is saying in the *Four Quartets* and how he is saying it. No two readers will see precisely the same meaning in a poem (novel, play, painting, sculpture, symphony, etc.) or react in precisely the same way, nor should they. However, some interpretations really *are* better than others. Some explications are based on misunderstandings or, worse still, on the critic's imposition of her values, emotions, and ideas onto the text. I shall endeavor to avoid these traps. I leave to readers to judge how far I have succeeded in avoiding the errors that I have (perhaps arrogantly) attributed to others.

INTRODUCTION

The Writing of the Four Quartets

Today, we usually read *Burnt Norton*, *East Coker*, *The Dry Salvages*, and *Little Gidding* in a single volume, or as a separate section of the Collected Poems, under the title *Four Quartets*. This naturally leads to the assumption that they were from the start envisaged and planned as one work. However, this is not so.

The idea for a poem structured similarly to *The Waste Land* developed from writing the play *Murder in the Cathedral* (1935). At the prompting of George Bell, the Bishop of Chichester, Eliot worked with producer E. Martin Browne on the pageant play *The Rock* (1934). Bell then asked Eliot to write another play for the Canterbury Festival in 1935, and Eliot agreed, provided Browne once again produced. The first performance was on June 15, 1935, in the Chapter House of Canterbury Cathedral. As frequently happens in production, the original text was significantly cut and revised. In 1953, Eliot recalled:

> There were lines and fragments that were discarded in the course of the production of *Murder in the Cathedral*. "Can't get them over on the stage," said the producer, and I humbly bowed to his judgment. However, these fragments stayed in my mind, and gradually I saw a poem shaping itself round them: in the end it came out as "Burnt Norton."

Burnt Norton was first published in the 1936 edition of *Collected Poems 1909–1935*.

The second poem, *East Coker*, finished in early 1940, was published in the U.K. in the Easter edition of the *New English Weekly* and in the U.S. in the May issue of the *Partisan Review*. In September, the poem was issued separately by Faber and Faber, the firm for which Eliot worked. Surprisingly, it sold 12,000 copies, drawing from Eliot the ironic comment that the poem could not have been very good if so many people had liked it.

It was while writing this poem that Eliot had the idea of composing a quartet of poems, although it was not until later that he explained his conception:

> [T]hese poems are all in a particular set form which I have elaborated, and the word 'quartet' does seem to me to start people on the right track for understanding them ('sonata' in any case is too musical). It suggests to me the notion of making a poem by weaving in together three or four superficially unrelated themes: the 'poem' being the degree of success in making a new whole out of them. (Letter to John Hayward, Sep. 3, 1942)

World War II began on September 1, 1939. Eliot started working on the third poem despite the disruption that this caused to his own life (he served as a watchman at the Faber and Faber building during the London Blitz and spent more time lecturing across Great Britain). *The Dry Salvages* was published in February 1941 in *The New English Weekly* and in book-form by Faber later in the year.

Eliot immediately began work on a fourth poem, *Little Gidding*, the site of Ferrar's religious community to whose chapel Eliot had made a personal pilgrimage in May 1936. However, by this time, Eliot's health was poor, and he stayed in Shamley Green in Surrey to recuperate. Perhaps because of a combination of ill-health and the war, he was dissatisfied with each draft. By September 1941, he stopped writing and focused on his lecturing. It was not until September 1942 that the last poem was published in book-form by Faber.

Eliot had originally contemplated the title *Kensington Quartets* to commemorate his time living in Kensington. However, *Four Quartets* was published as a whole by Harcourt, Brace & Co. in New York on May 11, 1943, and by Faber in London in 1944 with the explanation that, though they had initially been published separately, "The author ... had always intended them to be published as one volume, and to be judged as a single work." *Four Quartets* was first included with Eliot's other works in the U.S.A. in *Complete Poems and Plays* (1952) and in the U.K. in *Complete Poems 1909–62* (1963).

Lyndall Gordon draws attention to the autobiographical nature of the poems:

> The actual years in which he visited the scenes of Four Quartets [...] were years of upheaval, torn between nostalgia for unfulfilled love and the fury of tormented conscience. At the core of *Four Quartets* are the compacted memories of four years during which Eliot's new life was taking a decisive shape. (127)

A "new life" had opened up for Eliot after his 1927 conversion to Anglicanism, following which he had taken a vow of chastity. The "upheaval" in his life sprang from his separation from his erratic and possibly psychotic wife Vivienne and the reappearance in his life of Emily Hale (1891-1969), with whom he may still have been in love. Both women are present in *Four Quartets*. Hale is the narrator's unnamed companion in *Burnt Norton*. Vivienne makes no physical appearance, but as John Worthen explains, she is the dominant presence in the poem, "[N]othing in Eliot's last four major (and primarily religious) poems *Four Quartets* is now so compelling as their [...] confession of the guilt and remorse he experienced because of his marriage and how he had ended it" (187).

Four Quartets: **In a Nutshell**

Man is mortal: we are born, we live, and we will die. The Bible tells us, "The days of our years are threescore years and ten; and if by reason of strength they be fourscore years, yet is their strength labour and sorrow; for it is soon cut off, and we fly away" (*Psalms* 90:10, KJV). According to the Guinness Book of Records, "The greatest fully authenticated age to which any human has ever lived is 122 years 164 days by Jeanne Louise Calment [1875-1997]." That seems to be the upper limit because the cells in the body lose the ability to renew themselves. While great strides have been made in recent times to enable more people to live longer than they would have in earlier centuries, there is no indication that the upper limit can be extended.

Knowing ourselves to be mortal is arguably the most important thing a human being will ever learn. Therefore, one would expect that the moment we first understood that we are going to die would be pretty memorable. Strangely, it is not generally so. I can remember the Coronation Party for Queen Elizabeth II in 1953 and my first day at school a few years later, but I cannot pinpoint the moment I understood the terms of my sojourn on this planet.

Speaking of the planet, the Earth is about 4.5 billion years old, which is when the Solar System formed. For comparison, the age of the Universe is approximately 13.8 billion years. Of course, there are probably other universes, so that takes us into the realm of infinity. Suddenly, my 70 or so years look pretty insignificant.

Now we all know this, but we live our lives in denial of it. As Albert Camus (1913-1960) comments, "one will never be sufficiently surprised that everyone lives as if no one 'knew'" (*The Myth of Sisyphus*, 15). Our days are full of work, appointments, plans, obligations. These we remember, but death we tend to erase (or repress) from our consciousness. Of course, it tends to intrude itself every so often, when a friend or loved one dies or when we are seriously ill or in a life-threatening accident. But for the most part, we go through our everyday lives on autopilot, dealing as best we can with practicalities and avoiding existential questions.

That is all very well until, right out of the blue, we suddenly remember our mortality in contrast to the infinity of the multiverse. Camus describes such moments which can happen "on a street corner or in a restaurant's revolving door" (Ibid 12). The consequence is our sudden awareness that this world has no meaning that transcends it (or, at least, no meaning that humans can know, which amounts to the same thing). As a result, the entire superstructure of our day-to-day lives collapses like a stage set:

> Rising, streetcar, four hours in the office or the factory, meal, streetcar, four hours of work, meal, sleep, and Monday Tuesday Wednesday Thursday Friday and Saturday according to the same rhythm—this path is easily followed most of the time [… A] day comes when a man notices and says that he is thirty. Thus he asserts his youth. But simultaneously he situates himself in relation to time. He takes his place in it. He admits that he stands at a certain point on a curve that he acknowledges having to travel to its end. He belongs to time, and by the horror that seizes him, he recognizes his worst enemy. Tomorrow, he

was longing for tomorrow, whereas everything in him ought to reject it" (Ibid, 12-14)

Inevitably, this recalls the lament of Prufrock:

> I grow old ... I grow old ...
> I shall wear the bottoms of my trousers rolled.

> Shall I part my hair behind? Do I dare to eat a peach?
> I shall wear white flannel trousers, and walk upon the beach.
> I have heard the mermaids singing, each to each.
> I do not think that they will sing to me.
> ("The Love Song of J. Alfred Prufrock")

The time-trapped traveler is in an absurd position: the human need for meaning is confronted by a universe that is silent. When he wrote *Four Quartets*, Eliot was in his fifties; mortality was knocking on the door.

Nihilism is the natural reaction to the apparent meaninglessness of life. It is the reaction of Eliot's Sweeney in his dialogue with Doris:

> Birth, and copulation, and death.
> That's all the facts when you come to brass tacks:
> Birth, and copulation, and death.
> I've been born, and once is enough.
> ("Fragment of an Agon")

The logical conclusion of nihilism is suicide. Indeed, Camus begins *The Myth of Sisyphus* with the deliberately provocative assertion, "There is but one truly serious philosophical problem, and that is suicide" (1). Camus emphatically rejected suicide as a solution to the impasse of absurdity, but he likewise rejected the irrational leap of faith to belief in a God, all-knowing and all-loving, that had been the solution offered by Søren Kierkegaard (1813-1855). To Camus, both of these (nihilism and irrational hope) were mere evasions. He found the freedom of living in a meaningless universe in itself invigorating. It allowed humans the freedom to give life meaning without having to rely on a transcendent being or trying to construct meaningfulness by piling up material possessions on earth. Thus, "Assured of his temporary limited freedom, of his revolt devoid of future, and of his moral consciousness, he lives out his adventure within the span of his lifetime" (Ibid 66).

That is not a solution for everyone. Moreover, Camus might be wrong about the silent universe. As Colin Wilson (1931-2013) explains:

> [T]he main insight of all mystical experiences is obviously a sense of *meaning* – a feeling that the universe is not just an accidental conglomeration of matter, the chance result of some unexplainable big bang, but has the same kind of overall pattern and purpose that we can perceive in living organisms [...]

Mystical experiences invariably seem to instil [sic] courage and optimism" (*Beyond the Occult*, 51-52).

In *Four Quartets*, Eliot explores the possibility that humanity is not time-trapped. Following the hint of a chance moment of heightened consciousness experienced while walking in the gardens of Burnt Norton, he speculates on the possibility that there is a timeless pattern into which our time-limited lives meaningfully fit.

Reflecting his recent conversion to High Church Anglicanism, Eliot finally locates meaning in the sacrifice of Jesus Christ, which secured for mortal man eternal life. Having explored a number of situations in which humans can glimpse the experience of being both in and outside of time, he concludes that the ultimate example of this paradox is the incarnation. Christ was both man and God; He was both within and outside of historical time; Christ died to give humanity eternal life. Joel Edmund Anderson puts it well:

> *The Four Quartets* is Christian mystical poetry that contemplates the intersection of the fleeting moments within time to the ever-present now of eternity, with Christ as the still point, the spiritual center, within time, around which all of time and history revolves, and through which we experience union with the divine. ("T. S. Eliot's 'Four Quartets': Burnt Norton")

Four Quartets: An Overview

> Tradition is a matter of much wider significance. It cannot be inherited, and if you want it you must obtain it by great labour. It involves, in the first place, the historical sense, which we may call nearly indispensable to anyone who would continue to be a poet beyond his twenty-fifth year; and the historical sense involves a perception, not only of the pastness of the past, but of its presence; the historical sense compels a man to write not merely with his own generation in his bones, but with a feeling that the whole of the literature of Europe from Homer and within it the whole of the literature of his own country has a simultaneous existence and composes a simultaneous order. This historical sense, which is a sense of the timeless as well as of the temporal and of the timeless and of the temporal together, is what makes a writer traditional. (T. S. Eliot, "Tradition and the Individual Talent," 1919)

Eliot visited the three English locations in *Four Quartets* between 1934 and 1937, and in 1936 he crossed the Atlantic and subsequently visited various places in his homeland. In each place, he appears to have had what I will term a peak experience in this guide – a glimpse of a broader spiritual reality behind mundane, day-to-day existence. It is these personal experiences where Eliot sensed the timeless intrude into chronological time that the poet is exploring to understand the way "history is a pattern / Of timeless moments" (*Little Gidding* (739-740).

Burnt Norton

Norton House, near the village of Ashton-sub-Edge and the town of Chipping Campden in the beautiful Cotswolds (Gloucestershire, England), has a dramatic history. Sir William Keyt, 3rd Baronet (1688-1741) was a British landowner and Member of Parliament from 1722 to 1735. He married Anne Tracy in 1710. In 1716, Keyt acquired Norton House near Chipping, built a new mansion on adjacent land, and laid out an extensive garden. The total expenditure on the house and gardens was reputed to be £10,000. He then left his wife for her maid, Molly Johnson, with whom he went to live at Norton. According to local legend, when he first showed the manor house to her, she commented, 'What is a kite without wings?" so he added two large wings to the house. In 1741, however, Molly deserted him probably because of his heavy drinking. One night in September, almost certainly in a deranged state, Keyt caused a fire that engulfed the whole house. The fire was so powerful that one side of the original house was also scorched; hence, the property became known as Burnt Norton. Unsuccessful attempts were made to rescue Sir William, who was buried at the church Ashton-sub-Edge. In 1753, Sir Dudley Ryder bought the property and rebuilt the manor house, which his ancestors still own. The current owners began renovating the house and gardens around 2000.

In 1901-2, the house underwent extensive alterations and re-modeling by Sir Guy Dawber for the Earl of Harrowby. The gardens included a large parterre (i.e., a formal garden constructed on a level substrate, consisting of plant beds, typically in symmetrical patterns, separated and connected by paths) and terraces down the hillside. A new entrance court was established together with a fountain, terraces, orchard, and woodland walks.

Following his separation from his first wife, Vivienne, in February 1933, Eliot reconnected with Emily Hale, whom he had met and (probably) fallen in love with in 1912 when he was a graduate student of philosophy at Harvard. However, in 1914, Eliot had left America for Europe, and a year later, he had married Vivienne Haigh-Wood (1888-1947). In 1934, at the end of the academic year, Emily took unpaid leave from her post at Scripps College, California. She came to live with an American aunt and uncle, the Reverend and Mrs. Perkins, who had rented Stamford House on the High Street in the Cotswold village of Chipping Campden. Emily lived in the adjoining Stanley Cottage. Eliot was a frequent visitor, and in the late summer, he and Emily went to Burnt Norton, then an abandoned country house. Here the two explored the overgrown gardens. The air of decay in a place once so carefully kept had a profound effect on Eliot. The house itself does not significantly figure in the poem, but its extensive garden does. Hale seems to have been Eliot's poetic inspiration (at least for *Burnt*

Norton) – the Beatrice to his Dante.

To complete the story, it is clear that Eliot and Hale were still attracted to each other and may have been lovers had Eliot not remained legally married. She appears to have wanted to marry him, but although Eliot never saw Vivienne following their separation, his religious beliefs made divorce impossible. In 1935, Hale returned to the States, where she appears to have suffered an emotional breakdown so severe that in the following year, Eliot crossed the Atlantic to visit her. Hale recovered and took a new post in speech and drama at Smith College, Massachusetts. Hale and Eliot continued to spend summers together as guests of her aunt and uncle until 1939 when World War II put an end to transatlantic travel until 1946. Hale appears to have assumed that she and Eliot would marry after the death of Vivienne (which occurred in 1947), but he told her that he had no wish to do so. They infrequently met after that, and his last letter to Hale was in 1956. A year later, he married his secretary Esmé Valerie Fletcher (1926-2012).

Helen Gardener comments that "A formal garden is an admirable symbol for man's attempt to impose a pattern on his experience and to discipline nature" ("Four Quartets: A Commentary" Rajan Ed. 63). Eliot emphasizes the need for the individual to focus on the present moment and know there is a universal order. By understanding the nature of time and the order of the universe, humankind is able to recognize God and seek redemption. The present moment is the only time period that really matters because the past cannot be changed, and the future is unknowable. Memory is the key to understanding that the universe is based on order. Gardener continues, "it is an experience of a moment when one suddenly feels at home, accepted, free from anxiety […] It is not a moment that can be held, though it can be remembered. It is a moment that happens unexpectedly, as a grace, without the mind's preparing itself, or making any effort" (Ibid, 63). The poem also describes that although consciousness cannot be bound within time, humans cannot actually escape from time on their own – they can only achieve glimpses of what such an escape would be like. God is the only entity truly able to exist out of time and have knowledge of all times and places. However, humankind is still capable of redemption through belief in Him and His ability to save them from the bounds of the material universe.

East Coker

East Coker is a village three or four miles southwest of the town of Yeovil in Somerset. Rajan states that it is "a village not far from the sea" ("The Unity of the Quartets" in Rajan Ed. 82), but it is in reality almost twenty miles north of the coast. From *A Sketch of the Eliot Family* (1887) by Walter Graeme Eliot (1857-1931), Eliot learned that his family had lived in East Coker for two hundred years. Eliot visited East Coker in August 1937, taking photographs, including some of the village church St. Michael's. East Coker was literally

Eliot's beginning. In leaving his own family for England, Eliot had initiated the circular movement that would also make the village his end when ashes were laid to rest in St Michael and All Angels' Church. A plaque dedicated to Eliot reads, "In my beginning is my end. Of your kindness, pray for the soul of Thomas Stearns Eliot, poet. In my end is my beginning."

The first Eliot to be recorded in Somerset was Edmund Elyot in 1417. The family was "well educated, highly respected, well-to-do members of the landed gentry of the shire, and certainly well connected" (*Sketch* 12). On April 23, 1649, Andrew Eliott (1627-1704) married Grace Woodier, who gave birth to a son, also named Andrew, on January 30, 1650. Grace was buried on February 8, 1652. In 1654, Andrew remarried a woman called Mary (1630-1720), and she gave birth to Emma, who was buried on March 8, 1661, and to Mary, who was baptized on January 11, 1662. The last record of the Eliot family in the village is Andrew Eliot's name in 1668. Evidently a Puritan, Andrew left for the Massachusetts Colony with his wife and children. The family settled in Beverley, Massachusetts, in 1669/70 and immediately joined the First Church of Beverley. His son, also called Andrew, was drowned off Cape Sables when his ship foundered on September 12, 1688.

In 1690, Andrew Eliot was elected the first town clerk of Beverley, and in 1692 he achieved a kind of fame by being appointed one of the jurors at the Salem Witch Trials. Later, together with the other jurors, he would sign a "Declaration of Regret for the Part Taken" in the conviction and execution of some of those charged with witchcraft. Andrew's epitaph on his gravestone in Beverley Church reads, "Here lyes ye body of Andrew Eliot, aged 76 years, departed this life March ye 1st 1703-4."

Many commentators state that Sir Thomas Elyot (c.1496-1546), the scholar who served Henry VIII, was an ancestor of the poet who lived at East Coker. I have been unable to either substantiate or disprove both claims. Thomas Elyot's father held lands in Wiltshire and Oxfordshire, and in 1523 he inherited estates in Cambridge from his cousin. East Coker, however, is in South Somerset. *A Sketch of the Eliot Family records*, "The only Eliots recorded as resident in Somerset, other than Andrew's immediate ancestors, appear to be the family of Hugh Eliot (or Elyot) of Bristol ..." (8).

This poem focuses on birth, life, and death through many generations. Life on the earth is an endlessly recurring succession of birth, growth, decay, and death. The cycle of the year progresses through the seasons, and the passing of the year is indicated in the night sky. There is no comfort in this pattern, however, since it denies human achievement. The metaphor of autumnal serenity is false when applied to man because experience does not bring wisdom. Humans grasp to find a pattern in existence that will convey meaning, but these attempts fail.

The Dry Salvages

The Eliot family came from New England, and it was there they returned each summer from June to September. Having stayed for several years at Hampton Beach, New Hampshire, Eliot's father had a summer home built at Eastern Point, near Gloucester on Cape Ann, Massachusetts. Eliot spent his first summer there at the age of eight and would do so for eighteen more summers. As John Worthen explains, "[he] loved the place: the great granite rocks, the wind, the sea, the sunlight. He became a devoted bird-watcher and also learned to sail" (5). Eliot frequently sailed near the Dry Salvages, so he would have been well aware that the rocks are dangerously hidden, hence the need for warning beacons. Probably because of the obscurity of this location, particularly to English readers, Eliot provides the following explanation of the setting, "The Dry Salvages – presumably *les trois sauvages* – is a small group of rocks, with a beacon, off the N.E. coast of Cape Ann, Massachusetts." The only time they are named is in the poem's title.

The poem begins at St. Louis on the Mississippi River and ends by recapitulating some of the experiences of the first two poems. "The river is a reminder of what we should like to forget, our bondage to nature" (Ibid 67). Sailing on the sea is used as a metaphor for the human condition, "a meaningless, perpetual flux, a repetition without a pattern, to which each separate voyage adds nothing but itself." (Ibid 68). There is no development either in individual lives or in the lives of the community. Humankind searches fruitlessly into the past and tries to predict the future. Each generation, the women pray for the safety of their menfolk out at sea. Humanity is captive to linear time, but the Annunciation gives hope that it will be possible to escape. We experience eternity through moments of revelation, but we can attain it only through the grace of God.

Little Gidding

Little Gidding is a village in Cambridgeshire that Eliot visited in 1936. It was the home of an informal religious community established in 1626 by Nicholas Ferrar (1592-1637). Having lost a considerable amount of money in the Virginia Company, Ferrar withdrew from the world, taking his extended family to the virtually deserted village of Little Gidding. There, he lived with his mother; his brother John Ferrar, his wife Bathsheba and their children; and his sister Susanna, her husband John Collett, and their children. The community was not entirely cut off from the world, and its members took no vows nor conformed to any written rule. Members simply lived in strict adherence to Christian worship in accordance with the Book of Common Prayer and the Anglo-Catholic heritage of the Church of England. The community endured for two decades after Ferrar's death until the deaths of his brother and sister in 1657.

In 1633 and 1642, Charles I visited the community. Legend says that in 1646 he returned after the defeat of Royalist forces at Naseby, fleeing Parliamentary troops who broke up the community in their search for the king. Eliot's concern throughout the poem is the destruction of Europe's political, cultural, and religious traditions.

In this quartet, Eliot resolves the themes of the first three poems and speaks of spiritual renewal. Love alone, he concludes, can release us from our earthly desires. However, the love to which he refers is not a human movement or emotion, but the Divine Love that was a gift of Pentecost. The poem is about the intersection of time and eternity in this Love. God's love allows humankind to redeem itself and escape the tyranny of mortality through purgation by fire.

Divine Love is the theme of the lyric. William Laud explains, "The fires which have flamed and glowed throughout the poem here break out and declare their nature. Man cannot help loving; his choice is between the fire of self-love and the fire of the love of God [...] For when the fire and strength of the soul is sprinkled with the blood of the Lamb, then its fire becomes a fire of light, and its strength is charged with the strength of triumphing love, and will be fitted to have a place among those flames of love that wait about the throne of God."

Structure of the *Quartets*

Each quartet focuses on a place with its own particular importance to human history and uses each location to propose a series of ideas about spirituality and meaningful experience. *Burnt Norton* focuses on a transcendent experience in a rose garden, which is associated with the element air. *East Coker* focuses on the fields and lanes around a village associated with the element earth. In *The Dry Salvages* the element is water, and in *Little Gidding* it is fire. Each poem has five movements

FOUR QUARTETS

In music, the term 'quartet' describes music composed to be performed by four different instruments. In his 1942 essay "The Music of Poetry," Eliot wrote, "There are possibilities of transitions in a poem comparable to the different movements of a symphony or a quartet."

The poem begins with two epigraphs taken from the fragments of the pre-Socratic Greek philosopher Heraclitus (c.535-475 BCE):

τοῦ λόγου δὲ ἐόντος ξυνοῦ ζώουσιν οἱ πολλοί
ὡς ἰδίαν ἔχοντες φρόνησιν
(Though wisdom is common, the many live as if they have
wisdom of their own)
ὁδὸς ἄνω κάτω μία καὶ ὡυτή
(The way upward and the way downward is one and the same)

Originally, these epigrams appeared on the title page of the first British edition of *Burnt Norton*. Since the *Four Quartets* were published together, they have been placed before the title page to the first poem indicating that they have a thematic link to the work as a whole.

A more literal rendition of the first epigram reads, "Although the Word [*Logos*] is common to all, most people live as though each one had an understanding peculiarly his own." For Eliot (though obviously not for Heraclitus), the Word *is* Christ. The *Gospel of John* begins:

In the beginning was the Word, and the Word was with God, and the Word was God. The same was in the beginning with God. All things were made by him; and without him was not any thing made that was made. In him was life; and the life was the light of men. And the light shineth in darkness; and the darkness comprehended it not [...] And the Word was made flesh, and dwelt among us, (and we beheld his glory, the glory as of the only begotten of the Father,) full of grace and truth. (1:1-5 & 14, KJV)

Christ is the ultimate unifying principle of creation, but most did not (and still do not) recognize him. Their own particular understanding gets in the way of seeing the truth.

Eliot also gives the second epigram a Christian meaning. Joel Edmund Anderson explains, "In order to achieve union with Christ (the way up), one must die to oneself (the way down). There is only one way—and that way consists both of dying to self and rising with Christ" (op. cit.).

BURNT NORTON (1937)

Preparing to Read

I understand that you are probably anxious to read the text (or, if you have already done so, to reread it). However, I want to urge patience. Imagine an athlete running 100m without doing a warm-up. That would be a recipe for a pulled muscle and a 'did not finish,' or at best for a slow time. Of course, *Four Quartets* is much more like a marathon than a sprint, but even marathon runners warm up!

Trust me: to understand these poems, you will have to enter into the experience of them. Simply reading what Eliot wrote is not going to be enough. So spend some time reflecting on the following. How you do this is entirely up to you. You might sit in silent thought, write in a personal journal, or hold a discussion in a reading circle.

1. Have you ever had the experience of suddenly being thrown back into the past? What I mean is, have you ever been prompted by a sight, a smell, a taste, a touch, or a sound so vivid that you were propelled into reliving an experience? I am not talking about just triggering a memory here, though that is close to what I mean. If you have read the opening book of *Remembrance of Things Past: Swann's Way* (1913) by Marcel Proust (1871-1922), you will recall the description of how the narrator is thrown back into his childhood at Combray by the taste of a cake dipped in tea:

> And suddenly the memory returns. The taste was that of the little crumb of madeleine which on Sunday mornings at Combray (because on those mornings I did not go out before church-time), when I went to say good day to her in her bedroom, my aunt Léonie used to give me, dipping it first in her own cup of real or of lime-flower tea. The sight of the little madeleine had recalled nothing to my mind before I tasted it; perhaps because I had so often seen such things in the interval, without tasting them, on the trays in pastry-cooks' windows, that their image had dissociated itself from those Combray days to take its place among others more recent; perhaps because of those memories, so long abandoned and put out of mind, nothing now survived, everything was scattered; the forms of things, including that of the little scallop-shell of pastry, so richly sensual under its severe, religious folds, were either obliterated or had been so long dormant as to have lost the power of expansion which would have allowed them to resume their place in my consciousness. But when from a long-distant past nothing subsists, after the people are dead, after the things

are broken and scattered, still, alone, more fragile, but with more vitality, more unsubstantial, more persistent, more faithful, the smell and taste of things remain poised a long time, like souls, ready to remind us, waiting and hoping for their moment, amid the ruins of all the rest; and bear unfaltering, in the tiny and almost impalpable drop of their essence, the vast structure of recollection.

And once I had recognized the taste of the crumb of madeleine soaked in her decoction of lime-flowers which my aunt used to give me (although I did not yet know and must long postpone the discovery of why this memory made me so happy) immediately the old grey house upon the street, where her room was, rose up like the scenery of a theatre to attach itself to the little pavilion, opening on to the garden, which had been built out behind it for my parents (the isolated panel which until that moment had been all that I could see); and with the house the town, from morning to night and in all weathers, the Square where I was sent before luncheon, the streets along which I used to run errands, the country roads we took when it was fine. And just as the Japanese amuse themselves by filling a porcelain bowl with water and steeping in it little crumbs of paper which until then are without character or form, but, the moment they become wet, stretch themselves and bend, take on colour and distinctive shape, become flowers or houses or people, permanent and recognisable, so in that moment all the flowers in our garden and in M. Swann's park, and the water-lilies on the Vivonne and the good folk of the village and their little dwellings and the parish church and the whole of Combray and of its surroundings, taking their proper shapes and growing solid, sprang into being, town and gardens alike, from my cup of tea. ("Overture")

You *will* have had experiences like this. Describe at least one.

2. Search your memory for something in the past that you did not do – to coin a phrase from Robert Frost for a road that, for some reason, you did not take. We all have so many of these, most of them pretty trivial. However, some of the things we did not do changed our lives and will haunt us for the rest of our lives. You *will* have had experiences like this. Describe at least one.

3. Have you ever been in an old place (a ruined castle or house, or perhaps a derelict garden) and wondered what it was like in the past? Have you ever 'seen' that past vividly? In 1901, two British friends, Anne Moberly and Eleanor Jourdain, on holiday in France visited Versailles. They claimed actually to have

walked back into the days of Marie Antoinette, where they saw people in period costumes and some structures that had not existed since 1789. However, you do not have to believe in time travel to know how vividly the memory can recreate a past time. You *will* have had experiences like this. Describe at least one.

4. Visualization is a technique used a lot by sports psychologists. It involves getting the athlete to visualize an event in advance. Canadian bobsledder Lyndon Rush describes how for the four years between the 2010 and 2014 Olympics, he would see the track in his mind and visualize going around the turns. Think of something in your future that you are currently visualizing – literally seeing yourself as you will be (or at least as you want yourself to be) in the future. You *will* have experiences like this. Describe at least one.

Part I, Lines 1 – 17 ("Time present ... I do not know.")

Notes

"All time is unredeemable" (5) – 'Unredeemable' (or 'irredeemable') means: not able to be recovered or reformed; impossible to correct, improve or change; not able to be saved or liberated (especially from sin). If "all time is eternally present," then the past and the future have no independent existence; they are nothing more than an imaginative creation of the human mind operating in the present moment. The speaker does not say that this is so; he simply raises the possibility.

The word "unredeemable" calls to mind *Ephesians* 5.15-16, "See then that ye walk circumspectly, not as fools, but as wise, *redeeming the time*, because the days are evil" (KJV), and also the assertion by the young Prince Hal (the future Henry V):

> I'll so offend to make offense a skill,
> *Redeeming time* when men think least I will.
> (Shakespeare, *King Henry IV Part 1*, Act 1 Scene 2)

Hal is spending his time building a reputation as an ill-governed youth so that when he inherits the crown and shows his true qualities of maturity, courage, and judgment, people will be pleasantly surprised. Perhaps Eliot had this statement in mind when he decided to use the word "unredeemable," which is relatively uncommon. Eliot will be concerned later in the poem with the human inability to resolve the failures of one's lifetime and the horrors of history. We should also remember Heraclitus, "No man ever steps in the same river twice, for it's not the same river and he's not the same man." There is literally no going back.

The word "unredeemable" inevitably reminds the reader of Christ the Redeemer. Jesus Christ was born with a specific mission: to pay with his life for the remission of our sins and so earn us, by his sacrifice, an eternal life we could not ourself earn:

> For the grace of God that bringeth salvation hath appeared to

all men, Teaching us that, denying ungodliness and worldly lusts, we should live soberly, righteously, and godly, in this present world; Looking for that blessed hope, and the glorious appearing of the great God and our Saviour Jesus Christ; Who gave himself for us, *that he might redeem us from all iniquity*, and purify unto himself a peculiar people, zealous of good works. These things speak, and exhort, and rebuke with all authority. Let no man despise thee. (*Titus* 2:11-15, KJV)

And again:

[The Father] hath made us meet to be partakers of the inheritance of the saints in light: Who hath delivered us from the power of darkness, and hath translated *us* into the kingdom of his dear Son: In whom *we have redemption through his blood*, even the forgiveness of sins: Who is the image of the invisible God, the firstborn of every creature. (*Colossians* 1: 12-16, KJV)

"abstraction" (6) – An idea or concept that exists only in the mind – in this case, the part of the mind that controls memory.

"we [...] your mind" (12 & 15) – Even if the reader does not know that the genesis of this poem was a visit that Eliot made to a ruined garden with Emily Hale, it is clear that the speaker is addressing a companion with whom he shares past experiences. At the same time, the reader takes on the role of this anonymous companion because the narrator knows that the reader will empathize with what he is saying. The narrator and the reader have also shared past experiences because they are both human, and the experience of regret for the road not taken is universal.

In terms of literature, these opening lines put me in mind of Robert Frost's poems "The Road Not Taken" and "Stopping by Woods on a Snowy Evening," each of which describes a decision made in the present moment that will have consequences for the protagonist's life. Since both poems are in the public domain, here they are.

The Road Not Taken

Two roads diverged in a yellow wood,
And sorry I could not travel both
And be one traveler, long I stood
And looked down one as far as I could
To where it bent in the undergrowth;

Then took the other, as just as fair
And having perhaps the better claim,
Because it was grassy and wanted wear;
Though as for that, the passing there

Had worn them really about the same,

And both that morning equally lay
In leaves no step had trodden black
Oh, I kept the first for another day!
Yet knowing how way leads on to way,
I doubted if I should ever come back.

I shall be telling this with a sigh
Somewhere ages and ages hence:
Two roads diverged in a wood, and I,
I took the one less traveled by,
And that has made all the difference.

Stopping by Woods on a Snowy Evening

Whose woods these are I think I know.
His house is in the village, though;
He will not see me stopping here
To watch his woods fill up with snow.

My little horse must think it's queer
To stop without a farmhouse near
Between the woods and frozen lake
The darkest evening of the year.

He gives his harness bells a shake
To ask if there's some mistake.
The only other sound's the sweep
Of easy wind and downy flake.

The woods are lovely, dark, and deep,
But I have promises to keep,
And miles to go before I sleep,
And miles to go before I sleep.

Commentary

These lines read beautifully. In 1827, the English poet Samuel Taylor Coleridge (1772-1834) is reported to have said, "Prose = words in their best order; – poetry = the *best* words in the best order" (Henry Nelson Coleridge, *Specimens of the Table Talk of the Late Samuel Taylor Coleridge*, 1835). If that is true, then these lines are definitely poetry! The use of repetition is evocative. Even at first reading, when I had no idea what was being said, there was something magical, almost incantatory, about *the way it was being said.* Surprisingly, since the ideas on the nature of time are pretty complex, the diction is simple, with the possible exception of the unusual word "unredeemable."

We tend to assume that 'time' is the same as 'chronology'; that is, that time is a series of equidistant points (call them seconds, hours, weeks, years, decades, centuries, etc.) on a line along which the present moves in one direction only. In this model, the present is the only reality because only the present actually exists. The past we perceive as a series of events connected by cause and effect arranged in order of their occurrence. Thus, according to the Greek philosopher Aristotle, a story must have a beginning, middle, and end. A sense of chronology allows us to construct a timeline of events (e.g., The American War of Independence, the Covid Pandemic of the early 2020s, or our own lives). Chronology or duration is strictly linear; it moves only one way, and humans are effectively trapped in this movement. The future will be a series of equidistant points and events linked by cause and effect, but it has not happened yet.

In the linear time model (chronology, duration, or fixed time field), our lives begin with birth and end with death – a rather disturbing truth about which most people spend their time trying not to think. We can only ever occupy one position, the present, on our personal timeline, which fits neatly into the broader timeline of human history. Our position is entirely determined by the forward movement of time (yesterday, today, tomorrow) over which we have no control.

In contrast to this view of time, St. Augustine wrote, "Who shall lay hold upon the mind of man, that it may stand and see that time with its past and future must be determined by eternity, which stands and does not pass, which has in itself no past or future." Obviously, if we were to exist in eternity, then duration would cease to have any meaning, just as the concept of infinity means that time and space have no meaning. In eternity, we would reach a still point. However, humans are incapable of experiencing eternity or even of really understanding it since it is so different from our conception of time as a fixed field. (For example, I find it impossible to conceive of infinity. The best I can do is to think of it as a whole lot of 'finity' – like trillions of years.)

It is vital to bear in mind that, when Eliot wrote *Four Quartets*, there had been a great deal of speculation about the nature of time for several decades. This speculation spanned the range of thought from the scientific approach to parapsychology and the occult. Albert Einstein (1879-1955), in his revolutionary General Theory of Relativity (1915), explained how gravity affects the fabric of space-time. Specifically, since gravity affects light (bends it, for example), the speed of light is not constant, and therefore time is not constant. (It turns out that for astronauts in orbit, time is slower than for people on earth. Technically, they experience a time dilation of around -0.00002646 seconds every day.) At the same time, parapsychologists and occultists investigated a variety of psychic phenomena that appeared to call in question the concept of linear time (e.g., precognition and time-slips).

The author J. B. Priestley (1894-1984) was perhaps the most famous English writer on the concept of time in the twentieth century. Priestley began from his own experiences of a different kind of time than the usual linear model of birth and life, leading inexorably to death and extinction. He wrote of glimpses in which he had perceived a reality deeper and more permanent than the everyday world. These experiences were generated by memories of the past. These were so vivid that they engendered in Priestley a feeling of timelessness as if what was glimpsed were happening now, not in the past at all. He wrote:

> [...] on these occasions I have been recalling a person or a scene as clearly and as sharply as I could, and then there has been, so to speak, a little click, a slight change of focus, and for a brief moment *I have felt as if the person or scene were not being remembered but were really there still existing*, that nobody, nothing, had gone. I can't make this happen; either it happens or it doesn't [...] (*Over the Long High Wall*, 1972)

Priestley sought to explain the apparent coexistence of past, present, and future within a secular framework. In contrast, Eliot would attempt to explain identical experiences and conclusions about the nature of time within the framework of his Christian faith. This, then, was the intellectual context in which *Four Quartets* was written.

In the opening lines of the poem, the voice we hear appears to be anonymous. For the moment, let us assume that he is male and speaks with the author's authority – which is not quite the same thing as saying that the voice in the poem is that of T. S. Eliot. This narrator explores a complex view of time that appears to confirm linear chronology. However, the first two sentences do contain the essential qualifiers "perhaps" and "If." This indicates that the narrator is exploring a hypothesis rather than presenting a fully formed theory. The seventh sentence will end with the frank disclaimer, "I do not know" (17). This hesitancy is vitally important to an understanding of *Four Quartets*. These poems are the record of meditations upon time, not (or at least not initially) a definitive statement of a philosophy of time. Throughout, ideas are explored and rejected or superseded, as though the narrator is speculating or examining an idea by thinking aloud. This seems important because the reader is being invited to share the narrator's speculations rather than listen to a lecture. It is not just important what the speaker's ideas are; it is equally important to learn how he came by them.

The speaker speculates that the past and the present are both present in time future, just as the future is "contained" in time past. That is obviously true in a number of ways that every reader will have experienced. At some point in the future, our past and our present will still exist in the form of memories of what *did* happen. In our present, the future already exists in our imagination. So, even though it has not happened yet, time future is, in a sense present ("contained"), in the past since it is the product of what has already happened. For example, in the past, we made plans and had aspirations about the future that existed in our imagination – in our minds. Also, in our present, we have memories of what *did* happen in the past and thoughts about what *might have* happened.

This line of thought leads to the conclusion that past and future come together only in the present moment. If this is true, the narrator suggests, "All time is unredeemable" (5). This means that time past, time present, and time future cannot be recovered or improved or repeated or saved. The only thing humans can do is to live in the moment because there is *only* the moment. Reality exists only in the present moment; everything else is a construct of the mind. There is no point in spending time thinking back to everything that might have happened in the past. Such a "world of speculation" (8) exists only in "abstraction" (6); it is an endless diversion. The same may be said of thinking back to the things that did happen in the past, some of which might give us pleasure, and others fill us with pain and regret. They are now no more real than speculation about what might have happened – our memories, for example, might be inaccurate. Both experiences point to the "one end, which is always present" (10). Everything that *has* happened and everything that *could* have happened are basically the same thing because the past is finished and exists only in the present. (Presumably, although the narrator does not explicitly say so, the same must be true of the future. Everything that *does* happen and everything that *could* happen are fundamentally the same thing because the future has not yet happened, and it exists only in the present.)

Returning to the qualifiers "perhaps" and "If," it follows that the reverse of the argument *may* be true. If the past and future *do* have some independent existence beyond the present and outside our minds, then we *do not* live in past-present-future coexistent time. If the past and present "Are" present in time future, that implies that time future already, in some sense, exists just as certainly as time past exists. Therefore, time *is* redeemable: we are not stuck in the present but can time-travel (which would explain the many well-authenticated examples of people experiencing time-slips). However, this would involve a timeless experience *within* time which sounds like an oxymoron. You would literally have to step out of linear time (duration) to make contact with the past (or possibly the future); that is, we would step out of time to experience a timeless moment in time. Humankind may only approach such an experience occasionally, accidentally, and fleetingly. To live in such deeper reality for more than moments would be intolerable – the mind, which is used to linear time only, could not cope with it. However, if it is not possible for humans to redeem time, that *is* possible through the grace of Jesus Christ who "gave himself for us, that he might *redeem* us from all iniquity" (*Titus* 2:14, KJV). Christ redeems man both for the sins committed during his life and Adam's sin that passes from generation to generation, making all men sinners from the moment they are born. All this is perhaps to get somewhat ahead of the text, but it is clearly foreshadowed by the narrator's use of the word "unredeemable" (5).

Everything the narrator says about past, present, and future seems true – if not particularly startling or original. We all know that our memories of the past are actually imaginative recreations that are likely to be inaccurate, and we all know what it is like to spend time exploring alternative scenarios in which things might have worked out better (or at least different) for us. We also know that the future plans we have in mind may or may not come to pass. We talk dismissively about people who are 'living in the past' or always 'daydreaming about the future' because it stops them from getting on with their lives in the everyday world of duration. That reminds me of Jay Gatsby in *The Great Gatsby* (1925) by F. Scott Fitzgerald (1896-1940). Having experienced a perfect summer of love with Daisy Fey before going off to fight in the First World War, Gatsby returns determined to recapture that feeling (i.e., to redeem the time), even though Daisy is now married and has a daughter. Gatsby's friend Nick Carraway, who narrates the story, tries to warn him that Daisy is no longer the young girl he fell in love with:

> "I wouldn't ask too much of her," I ventured. "*You can't repeat the past.*"
> "Can't repeat the past?" he cried incredulously. "Why of course you can!"
> He looked at me wildly, as if the past were lurking here in the shadow of his house, just out of reach of his hand. (Chapter 6)

Nick is right, of course: Daisy and Gatsby have both changed, and the world has moved on. There will be no recreating the past in the present. Then there are the people who spend their lives planning for the future whom we dismiss as dreamers. Once again, Gatsby is illustrative for he fantasizes about a life with Daisy in the future after she has left her husband. In oft-quoted lines near the end of the novel, Nick points to the tragic error which at once raises Gatsby above all the other characters (who are quite incapable of an idealized visualization of the future) and finally kills him:

> He had come a long way to this blue lawn, and his dream must have seemed so close he could hardly fail to grasp it. *He did not know that it was already behind* him [...] Gatsby believed in the green light, the orgiastic future that year by year recedes before us [...] So we beat on, boats against the current, borne back ceaselessly into the past. (Chapter 9)

Gatsby, equally obsessed by memories of the past, by endless speculation of what might have been and dreams of a future that will never happen, fails to live in the present. As summer ends, he suddenly realizes that he has not once used his mansion's magnificent swimming pool. Gatsby lives in a world of "abstraction [...] perpetual possibility [...] speculation" without realizing that the only time that is real is the present moment.

Ironically, no sooner has the poem's speaker established this 'truth' (at least to his own satisfaction) than he is distracted by memories of a road not taken. As often happens, a sense impression (in this case, something he hears) recalls the same sense impression from decades ago, and the narrator finds himself drawn back into the past. He says, "Footfalls echo in the memory" (11). The sound of his and his companion's footsteps as they walk around the garden at Burnt Norton triggers a memory of another garden in the past and a regret that "we" (i.e., the two of them) never went down one particular passage and never opened a particular door that would have led into the rose-garden.

The narrator appears both to be addressing his silent walking companion and the reader. He seems confident that both she and we will identify with the experience he describes, "My words echo / Thus in your mind" (14-15), the companion because she will recognize the incident and readers because we have had similar experiences. Inevitably, the speaker's tone is regretful: the rose-garden symbolizes the beautiful, a wonderful life experience that "we" (narrator, companion, and reader) never achieved. But perhaps it can be achieved now. All of this, of course, is the very reverse of what the speaker has just said about time past being "unredeemable." What he describes is no mere abstraction; it is not even a memory. The narrator is actually back in the past having stepped out of time to experience a timeless moment.

This must also seem familiar to every reader. Oh, those lost opportunities and how many hours we waste obsessing about and reliving them! The speaker anticipates that his words will resonate in the reader's mind. The reader will empathize with what he is saying. We can all think of decisions we took or events beyond our control that made all the difference to the course of our lives. Perhaps it was fear or shyness that held us back from the corridor and prevented us from opening the door, or maybe it was just chance. If only...

The comments of Stephen Spender on the relationship of poet and reader established in *Burnt Norton* and carried through the other quartets seem important here:

> [...] *the poet's ground of experience is the same as that of other men*, even though he happens to be a poet and to have had experiences which are – as are those of all men, to themselves – special to himself [...] *Like the reader's, his personal history is a sum of moments in time. Among these he has had experience of the intersection of time with timelessness.* The experience of timelessness is religious and not aesthetic, though art (as with the Chinese jar moving 'perpetually in its stillness') may be the occasion for it [...] The 'I' therefore of Eliot the man, who is growing old, provides the connection between the author of the poem and the reader [...] The poet appeals to the reader on the grounds of shared experience of living within time. This experience of being both bound to time and outside

it, is religious. However set Eliot may be on transforming this time-subject into poetry, he is equally set on persuading the reader – 'hypocrite lecteur' – that *he shares with him the fundamental religious situation of being both inside the particular moment and outside it*. (*T. S. Eliot*, 163-164)

All that the narrator says convinces us that whatever happened in that earlier garden must have been pretty significant. So what might it have been?

There is a school of critical thought that declares biography out of bounds to the literary critic. I am usually a loyal adherent of this school, and even more ironically, so was T. S. Eliot. However, in Eliot's case, he wrote so much out of his own emotional wounds that it seems churlish to ignore the obvious, which begins with Eliot's acknowledgment that the germ of the experience described in the poem was a visit he made to the gardens at Burnt Norton in the company of Emily Hale. Biographical evidence suggests that Eliot loved Hale in his youth but left America for Europe and ended their relationship (in which order is not clear). Later, when they reconnected, Hale wanted to marry Eliot but, perhaps still suffering the lacerations of his first marriage, or because he held the marriage vow to be inviolable while his first wife was still alive, Eliot did not wish to remarry. This may account for the narrator's obsession with "what might have been" (9) and "the passage we did not take" (12). Dwight Longnecker is undoubtedly correct when he points out that "Although the poems seem impossibly abstract, they are in fact, rooted in objective experience. *The key to understanding them is to understand those objective connecting points in biography and geography – time and place*" ("Listening to 'Burnt Norton'").

Memories have, then, been stirred, despite all the narrator has said about memories and regrets being merely abstract speculations. However, it remains to be seen "to what purpose" (15). An old bowl of rose-petal potpourri, dried and dead, represents the past memories that have been revivified (redeemed) by the visualization of a beautiful rose garden that he never visited, a rose garden in which the roses are alive again. The "dust on a bowl of rose-leaves" (16) has been disturbed by the stirred memory prompted by the sound of footfalls, but to what purpose? In a tone that is almost regretful, the speaker admits, "I do not know." The introduction of two broken lines (15 and 17) and the heavy 'd' alliteration suggest some emotional disturbance. The halting rhythm of the verse is very different from the calm, meditative opening. The narrator appears to be in uncharted waters. His situation is a little like that of Alice having fallen down the rabbit hole to find herself in Wonderland. He invites us (and his companion) to follow him as he explores.

Part I, Lines 17 – 46 ("Other echoes … is always present.")

Notes

"The deception of the thrush" (22) – This calls to mind "The Darkling Thrush"

(1900) by Thomas Hardy (1840-1928):

> I leant upon a coppice gate
>> When Frost was spectre-gray,
> And Winter's dregs made desolate
>> The weakening eye of day.
> The tangled bine-stems scored the sky
>> Like strings of broken lyres,
> And all mankind that haunted nigh
>> Had sought their household fires.
>
> The land's sharp features seemed to be
>> The Century's corpse outleant,
> His crypt the cloudy canopy,
>> The wind his death-lament.
> The ancient pulse of germ and birth
>> Was shrunken hard and dry,
> And every spirit upon earth
>> Seemed fervourless as I.
>
> At once a voice arose among
>> The bleak twigs overhead
> *In a full-hearted evensong*
>> *Of joy illimited*;
> An aged thrush, frail, gaunt, and small,
>> In blast-beruffled plume,
> Had chosen thus to fling his soul
>> Upon the growing gloom.
>
> So little cause for carolings
>> Of such ecstatic sound
> Was written on terrestrial things
>> Afar or nigh around,
> That I could think there trembled through
>> His happy good-night air
> *Some blessed Hope, whereof he knew*
>> *And I was unaware.*

The poem's narrator accepts the message of the thrush as embodying a knowledge superior to his own. Still, given the European war that was to happen in just sixteen years, an argument can be made that in doing so, he followed the deception of the thrush.

"unheard music" (27) – This is the first of several clear references to "Ode on a Grecian Urn" (1819) by the English Romantic poet John Keats (1795-1821). Here is the poem in full. Words and phrases which find an echo in Eliot's poem are italicized:

Thou still unravish'd bride of quietness,
   Thou foster-child of Silence and slow Time,
Sylvan historian, who canst thus express
   A flowery tale more sweetly than our rhyme:
What leaf-fring'd legend haunts about thy shape
   Of deities or mortals, or of both,
      In Tempe or the dales of Arcady?
What men or gods are these? What maidens loth?
   What mad pursuit? What struggle to escape?
      What pipes and timbrels? What wild ecstasy?

Heard melodies are sweet, but those unheard
   Are sweeter; therefore, ye soft pipes, play on;
Not to the sensual ear, but, more endear'd,
   Pipe to the spirit ditties of no tone:
Fair youth, beneath the trees, thou canst not leave
   Thy song, nor ever can those trees be bare;
      Bold lover, never, never canst thou kiss,
Though winning near the goal—yet, do not grieve;
   She cannot fade, though thou hast not thy bliss,
      For ever wilt thou love, and she be fair!

Ah, happy, happy boughs! that cannot shed
   Your leaves, nor ever bid the Spring adieu;
And, happy melodist, unwearied,
   For ever piping songs for ever new;
More happy love! more happy, happy love!
   For ever warm and still to be enjoy'd,
      For ever panting, and for ever young;
All breathing human passion far above,
   That leaves a heart high-sorrowful and cloy'd,
      A burning forehead, and a parching tongue.

Who are these coming to the sacrifice?
   To what green altar, O mysterious priest,
Lead'st thou that heifer lowing at the skies,
   And all her silken flanks with garlands drest?
What little town by river or sea shore,
   Or mountain-built with peaceful citadel,
      Is emptied of this folk, this pious morn?
And, little town, thy streets for evermore
   Will silent be; and not a soul to tell
      Why thou art desolate, can e'er return.

O Attic shape! Fair attitude! with brede

Of marble men and maidens overwrought,
With forest branches and the trodden weed;
    Thou, silent form, dost tease us out of thought
As doth eternity: Cold pastoral!
    When old age shall this generation waste,
        Thou shalt remain, in midst of other woe
Than ours, a friend to man, to whom thou say'st,
    "Beauty is truth, truth beauty"—that is all
        Ye know on earth, and all ye need to know.

Eliot also has in mind St John of the Cross, *Spiritual Canticle,* XIV-XV (emphasis added):

My Beloved is the mountains,
The solitary wooded valleys,
The strange islands,
The roaring torrents,
The whisper of the amorous gales;
The tranquil night
At the approaches of the dawn,
The *silent music,*
The murmuring solitude,
The supper which revives, and enkindles love.

"the unseen eyebeam crossed" (28) – Eliot borrows the phrase from the poem "*The Ecstasy*" by the English Metaphysical poet John Donne (1572-1631). Donne is describing two lovers looking into each other's eyes. Here are the first twelve lines with the relevant section italicized:

Where, like a pillow on a bed
    A pregnant bank swell'd up to rest
The violet's reclining head,
    Sat we two, one another's best.
Our hands were firmly cemented
    With a fast balm, which thence did spring;
Our eye-beams twisted, and did thread
    Our eyes upon one double string;
So to'intergraft our hands, as yet
    Was all the means to make us one,
And pictures in our eyes to get
    Was all our propagation.

"the roses / Had the look of flowers that are looked at" (28-29) – Compare, "To prepare a face to meet the faces that you meet" (*The Love Song of J. Alfred Prufrock*).

"the box circle" (32) – A box in a theater accommodates a small party. It has moveable seats, unlike the auditorium, where the seating is fixed in rows. Boxes are often on one or more levels (the circle) above the auditorium, so viewers look down upon the stage. In a formal garden, a box circle is a focal point in the garden's center formed by a low circular hedge of boxwood. Such gardens are usually square (or rectangular) with an entrance in the middle of each side of the square in the form of a path leading to what a person looking from the house's upper story would see as the exact center.

"the drained pool" (33) – There was a dry pool at Burnt Norton (search the Internet for photographs). There seems to have been a rectangular pool, quite deep and adjacent, a semi-circular fountain pool that was much shallower.

The "lotos rose" (36) – The lotus rose reminds us that the setting is a rose garden in England, but it also introduces the oriental theme. In the *Upanishads*, the lotus symbolizes purity:

> The Lotus Flower grows in the deep mud, far away from the sun. But, sooner or later, the Lotus reaches the light becoming the most beautiful flower ever. The Lotus flower is regarded in many different cultures, especially in eastern religions, as a symbol of purity, enlightenment, self-regeneration and rebirth. Its characteristics are *a perfect analogy for the human condition: even when its roots are in the dirtiest waters, the Lotus produces the most beautiful flower*. ("The Symbolic Meaning of the Lotus Flower," Institute for Asia and Asian Diasporas, Binghamton University)

Thus, the lotus rising out of a dried-up pool prefigures the reference to "release" and "*Erhebung*" in the next section.

"the leaves were full of children, / Hidden excitedly, containing laughter" (40-41) – John Worthen explains that the image of children in a garden or an orchard recurs in Eliot's poetry between 1918 and 1942 often linked with the smell of thyme or the sound of a waterfall. The children are always hidden (by a wall or foliage or falling water), their presence revealed only by the sound of their voices or laughter. He suggests the source of this image:

> The garden of the family house in St. Louis had been bounded by a brick wall, on the far side of which was the girls' school founded by Eliot's grandfather, the Mary Institute, its schoolyard shaded by 'a huge ailanthus tree'; *the children were regularly heard, hardly ever seen, 'always on the other side of the wall'*." (218)

Worthen goes on to speculate that the repeated references to children had "something to do with Eliot's longing for the children he had never had" (220). Given his wife Vivienne's physical and psychological problems, Eliot found it impossible to contemplate having children. In these lines, the children seem to represent lost innocence and the children that Eliot might have had if he had married Elizabeth Hale, with whom he had been romantically involved before he met Vivienne.

Commentary

As soon as the sound of footsteps recovers one memory, the experience of being in the ruined garden stirs "Other echoes" (7). These crowd into the minds of both the speaker and the reader. His invitation, "Shall we follow?" (8) reminds me of the opening of "The Love Song of J. Alfred Prufrock":

> Let us go then, you and I,
> When the evening is spread out against the sky
> Like a patient etherized upon a table;
> Let us go, through certain half-deserted streets,
> The muttering retreats
> Of restless nights in one-night cheap hotels
> And sawdust restaurants with oyster-shells:

There the reader is being invited to confront "an overwhelming question" about the nature of life by visiting the very poorest parts of the city. Here "we" (the narrator's silent companion and the reader) are being tempted out of the present into a past that does not seem to be either abstraction and speculation. That sounds weird but infinitely tempting.

We are called to search for other, related memories by the urging of a bird saying, "Quick [...] find them, find them." Just as the present sound of steps on the garden path has resonated in the mind, stirring memories, so now the chirping of a real bird appears to the speaker to be urging him to recover more memories connected to the garden in the past. It sounds a little like a scavenger hunt. The speaker refers to the "deception of the thrush" (21, 22). This may refer to the way some birds protect their chicks by pretending to be injured to draw predators away from their nests. That would seem to make sense. The "deception" refers back to the narrator's feeling at the *start* of the poem that memories are merely abstract speculations. The bird's invitation to enter an alternative past in which the two actually enter the rose garden may be no more than a diversion from reality. Unlike Thomas Hardy's thrush, which represents a sort of hope beyond human understanding, this thrush appears to be offering a false kind of hope by taking us away from the present. On the other hand, it may be the opening of a deeper reality.

I interpret the repeated pronoun "they" (30, 31) to refer to their former selves conjured up by the bird and thus present in the garden at Burnt Norton as "our guests" (30). They are walking "dignified, invisible, / Moving without pressure, over the dead leaves" (23-24) through the garden at Burnt Norton in the autumn heat. The dead leaves symbolize their forgotten past, perhaps their forgotten love. Then they are led down the rabbit hole of memory into "our first world" (21 &

22). This phrase is repeated twice, so it must be important. Inevitably, the words suggest that the memory involves a symbolic return to the Garden of Eden, with the narrator and his companion as the innocent lovers Adam and Eve. The bird is able to respond to the "music hidden in the shrubbery" that remains "unheard" by the two humans (27). The bird also sees "the unseen eyebeam crossed, for the roses / Had the look of flowers that the looked at" (29-30). I take this to mean that the bird can see the two former lovers in that past garden, looking into each other's eyes and looking at the roses. This was a time when the world appeared full of meaning and potential. The two lovers were at one with nature, experiencing it intensely. For the bird, the past young lovers are as real as the present middle-aged couple.

Now, effectively, two couples are walking together around the garden of the manor. They move "in a formal pattern" (31) since the garden is laid out that way, along the "empty alley, into the box circle" (32). This may be an image from the theater or garden design or a brilliant synthesis of the two. Either way, they come to a still point among the once immaculately trimmed boxwood hedges from which they can look down into "the drained pool" (33). In Eliot's poetry, lack of water symbolizes infertility and a spiritual thirst that, at least in the early poems, cannot be quenched.

The concept of pattern seems to be critical here. Burnt Norton had been a formal garden, and the design is evident even though it has been left unattended for years. The pattern has endured. It certainly is not timeless, but it still connects the garden that *is* with the garden that *was*. This seems to be the source of its power to take the narrator back to the "first world" that he shared with his companion – not in this garden but in another garden where the roses were alive with blossom.

The bird is able to respond to the "music in the shrubbery" that is "unheard" by the humans (27). The origin of this music is not entirely clear. It may be an actual memory or the music of the spheres. Is it simply that the bird is more sensitive than humans (literally open to wavelengths outside the capacity of the human ear as dogs are), and is hearing sound that vanished from human hearing decades ago? I think it is more likely that the music is related to the pattern of the garden. That pattern has captured the sound of music from former days and somehow 'recorded' it so that it still exists. This is not so fanciful. Every reader will have suddenly experienced 'hearing' a sound from years ago. Also preserved in the garden is "the unseen eyebeam [that was] crossed" between the two innocent lovers (28) in a moment so perfect that "the roses / Had the look of flowers that are looked at" (28-29). It appears that the man and woman were not only in love with each other but with the beauty of the world around them.

Once again, biography points to an obvious explanation, and it would be simply perverse to ignore it. Adam and Eve went naked and unashamed in Eden; their love was pure and unsullied by lust or sexual desire. That all ended when they ate of the fruit of the Tree of Knowledge and lost their innocence which they could never recover because, as a punishment, they were exiled into the fallen world. Eliot seems to be recalling the period in his relationship with Hale before he left for Europe. That must have been a golden time of young love (the parallel with Gatsby and Daisy's summer of love is clear) when everything seemed possible before his move to Europe and his marriage to Vivienne and all the complexities of life closed the door forever on that potential.

The contrast with the present could not be greater. Along with the image of Burnt Norton, the house destroyed by fire, the "dead leaves" (24) that litter the ground suggest death and the coming of winter (symbolizing death). Perhaps the narrator is aware of the gathering clouds of war. Perhaps he has in mind that his own death is coming ever closer and wonders whether the death of his mortal body will also mark the death of his spirit or soul. The "autumn heat" (25) is oppressive, for these are the dog days of summer, the hottest, most uncomfortable part of summer in the Northern Hemisphere. The heat accounts for the description of the air as "vibrant" since heat rising from the ground distorts the appearance of things. The overgrown and abandoned garden is a symbol of humanity's inability to build anything that is permanent. It also prefigures the wreckage of Western civilization on the eve of the Second World War – a sort of *déjà vu*, since *The Wasteland* reflected the same disintegration during World War I.

In the present, the two couples move through a former paradise now abandoned and neglected – a sort of Paradise Lost. They walk now "Along the empty alley" (32) that leads not to the rose garden but the pool. Once a place of magical purity, it is now empty, revealing its ugly "dry concrete, brown edged" (34). The speaker then describes a moment of insight in the garden. The reality of the empty pool is unattractive. Notice the repetition of "dry," which suggests death, and the "brown" concrete that recalls the dying leaves of autumn (34). But in the sunlight, it appears that the pool is full of water with a beautiful lotus rose "quietly, quietly" floating on its surface (36). The lotus rose is a traditional eastern symbol for the human soul climbing up out of the mud (symbolizing the material world) toward spiritual enlightenment. Is this an optical illusion created by the sunlight or a timeless moment in time? The implication seems to be that the narrator has had a glimpse of a past that still exists, and if that is true, he has experienced a reality beyond the constraints of duration.

Looking down, the narrator remembers seeing the younger selves of himself and his companion apparently "reflected in the pool" (38). The illusion or vision, a remembrance of time past, lasts but for a moment. A cloud obscures the sun and reveals the present reality. The abruptness is captured in a single line, "Then a cloud passed, and the pool was empty," delivered without emotion as a bald statement of fact (39). Thus, a beautiful but perhaps troubling moment of enlightenment has come out of the ruined garden at Burnt Norton. Something of the original garden pattern has remained despite its neglect, and that pattern has united past and present. Is the narrator's vision of the past selves of himself and his companion mere deception, or is it a meaningful vision? Is it a mere fabrication of the mind or a genuine spiritual experience? The narrator does not tell us, presumably because he is himself unsure.

At this point, the bird reverses its earlier call for the narrator to follow his memories, "Go, go, go, said the bird" (42). The explanation seems to be that "the leaves were full of children, / Hidden excitedly, containing laughter" (40-41). The image gives a delightful sense of childish innocence and innocence lost as we grow older. Perhaps these are the children the narrator never had because he and his companion did not enter the rose garden (i.e., did not marry). Perhaps they are simply voices that the narrator heard in his youth but never identified. In any case, they belong to an alternative past, and there may be yet other fantoms of the past waiting to be resurrected in the narrator's mind. The bird warns that "human kind / Cannot bear very much reality" (42-43), which seems to imply that what the speaker has experienced has been a real time-slip and not a mere abstraction. In linear time, at the age of fifty or so, he has had a glimpse of a reality beyond that of everyday duration. The implications of such an experience are mind-blowing. The speaker and his companion must leave the perfect garden of their memory and return to the derelict garden of Burnt Norton. I am reminded of William Faulkner, "The past is never dead. It's not even past" (*Requiem for a Nun*, 1951).

In the last three lines, the narrator draws a conclusion from the experience in the garden: it is only in the present that what *was*, what *might have been* and what *might be* can have any existence. Memories and imaginings connecting the individual to the past and the future offer an escape from the mundane everyday world into a reality that is often painful and of which humankind cannot bear too much. If this is true, then it is *not true* that "All time is unredeemable" (5).

Summary of Part I

The speaker describes a transcendent experience, a moment in time when the narrator experienced a sense of timelessness. That is, he was able to escape from the tyranny of linear time that normally dictates human life into a past that still exists. Memory is the key to this experience. Life seems to be merely a succession of random events, points on a timeline that do not have any form. As we recollect these events, however, memory forms them into a pattern, which suggests that they are in some way unbound by time. It is a fleeting glimpse that gives meaning to the otherwise meaningless life of man. The sense of heightened perception lasts for only an instant, nor is it completely understood, but it is a glimpse of a solution to the interface of chronology and eternity.

Part II, Lines 47 – 61 ("Garlic and sapphires ... among the stars.")

Notes

"Garlic" (47) – A member of the onion family used a lot to give flavor to cooking.

"sapphires" (47) – A precious gemstone commonly thought of as blue, though other colors occur. Sapphires are found in alluvial deposits (clay, silt, sand, or gravel) deposited in the past by running water.

"Garlic and sapphires in the mud" (47) – This is Eliot's take on the line, "*Tonnerre et rubis aux moyeux*" ["Thunder and ruby at the hubs"] from the poem, "*M'introduire dans ton histoire*" ["Introduce me into your story"] a poem by the French symbolist poet Stéphane Mallarmé (1842-1998) published in *Poésies* (1899).

"Clot" (48) – Form a coagulated mass around.

"axle-tree" (48) – A crossbar under an animal-drawn cart or wagon, with rounded spindles at each end upon which the wheels rotate.

"inveterate" (50) – An action or character trait that is longstanding, ingrained, deep-rooted and unlikely to change.

"Appeasing" (51) – Pacifying, conciliating, placating.

"the artery ... the lymph" (52-53) – Arteries are a system of elastic tubes that carry blood away from the heart to the cells, tissues, and organs of the body. If that movement stops, death results. The lymph is "a clear yellowish, slightly alkaline, coagulable fluid, containing white blood cells in a liquid resembling blood plasma, that is derived from the tissues of the body and conveyed to the bloodstream by the lymphatic vessels" (Dictionary.com).

"the moving tree" (55) – In 1680, King Charles II told Samuel Pepys (1633-1703) that while he was hiding in an oak tree in Boscobel Wood, in the county of Shropshire, a Parliamentarian soldier passed directly below it without seeing him. We only have his word for it. The incident will be referred to again in *Little Gidding*.

"the boarhound and the boar" (59) – "Once commonly found in many parts of Great Britain, the wild boar was strictly preserved in the royal forests during the medieval period for the benefit of the monarch and favoured noblemen. Boar were hunted by packs of large mastiff-type hounds at this time, and when cornered and held at bay were slaughtered using swords and spears – the heads being a highly sought-after delicacy for banquets. However, due to a combination of over-hunting, poaching and habitat loss, wild boar had become extinct in Britain by the end of the 17th century." (Davis Jones, "Wild Boar Hunting in Europe: A Brief History," Fieldsports. Web. Nov. 11, 2021) There is no generally recognized constellation representing either boar or boarhound.

Commentary

In this section, things get obscure because the narrator is speaking in metaphors. An "axel-tree" is not a tree at all. It is the beam across the underpart of a wagon to the end of which the wheels are fixed. If the wagon/car represents an individual and the movement of the wagon the individual's progress through life, then the clinging and accumulating mud suggests that life can be hard-going. The mud of life embeds itself around the wheels and even around the axle. Perhaps the carriage is literally stuck (embedded) axel-deep in the mud.

Along the way, the wheels churn up "Garlic [plants] and sapphires" in the mud (47). Presumably, these represent the wide range of experiences one encounters in life. Though we might see the garlic as common and worthless while sapphires are rare and precious, ironically, we might also see garlic as living, organic, and health-giving while sapphires are wholly lifeless, inanimate, and of little practical use. The word "Clot" (48), initially used to describe the accumulation of mud on the axle of the wagon/car, prefigures references to the circulation of the blood. The accumulation of life's debris in the veins slows the passage of the blood so that it turns from liquid into a gel-like substance, potentially forming a life-threatening blockage or blood clot.

The phrase "trilling wire" used in conjunction with the word "mud" would inevitably have evoked in anyone of Eliot's generation an image of the barbed wire strung across no man's land between the trenches in World War One. The trilling of the wire might be the sound of the wind vibrating the wire. By describing this wire as "in the blood," the narrator seems to be implying that the psychic damage of the war remains deep within even those who have forgotten the war itself. A similar metaphor follows: the skin of humans is marked by the "inveterate scars" of age-old battles, symbolizing the painful defeats that all humans suffer in their lives (50). Yet still, beneath the scar tissue, the blood flows – the life force remains strong, blocking out the pain, not allowing it to become overwhelming.

The "trilling wire" (49) sounds like a reference to telegraph wires that transmit unseen messages through electrical pulses. In the same way, the blood is alive, dancing along the arteries keeping the body going. The "trilling" in the blood might represent the messages sent along the nerves and/or the pulsing of the blood and the lymph containing the white blood cells that keep life going. Lymph may also mean the sap of a plant and a stream or spring of clear, pure water. It thus symbolizes the life force which drives on in humankind, flora, and the natural world.

In alchemy, there is a saying: 'As above, so below.' This expresses the belief that the macrocosm and the microcosm are linked: whatever happens on earth is reflected in the astral plane and vice versa. This idea is explored by the narrator, who notes that the life force in the human body is "figured in the drift of stars" (54). There is a mystical connection between the circulation of the blood in our veins and the movements of the entire universe through the cycle of the year. This again refers to the constellations and perhaps to a person's horoscope, which predicts that person's life. Constellations ascend and descend in the sky with the cycle of the seasons.

The reference to "the moving tree" is puzzling, but some history may help. In 1651, after the Royalist defeat at the Battle of Worcester, Charles (son of King Charles I) claimed that he climbed into the branches of an oak tree in Boscobel Wood to evade capture by his Parliamentary enemies. The ruse appears to have worked. After the monarchy was restored in 1660 with his coronation as Charles II, the incident was commemorated by a national holiday and the naming of a new constellation. Edmund Halley (1656-1742) 'discovered' the constellation, named it *Robur Carolinum* or "Charles's Oak," and explained that he did so, "In memory of the hiding place that saved Charles II of Great Britain etc., deservedly translated to the heavens forever." This was a clear illustration of the doctrine, 'As above, so below.' Sadly, Halley's new constellation never really caught on with astronomers, and it soon disappeared from view. The actual Royal Oak of Boscobel did not last much longer: sightseers during the seventeenth and eighteenth centuries cut so many pieces off as souvenirs that it died. Of course, T. S. Eliot knew all about this and expected his readers to know about it. Once one does, the difficulty of the lines all but vanishes.

The narrator changes perspective: he rises "above the moving tree," which may describe the movement of the constellations in the night sky throughout the year and/or the act of projecting the self above the tree. Either way, we are now looking down on the earth from above. The connection between our bodies and the stars enables us to "Ascend" from the mud into the glorious "summer in the tree" (55). Perhaps this is a reference back to the description in *Burnt Norton* of walking around the formal garden. There, the narrator implied that humanity is stuck in the dying days of autumn, just as he is stuck in the autumn of his life. Now, our connection to the stars raises us from "the sodden floor"(58) to take our place among "light upon figured leaf," which is suggestive of spring or summer (57). This new perspective recalls earlier when he looked down on the pool from the "box circle."

The narrator looks down upon life on earth from the point of view of someone who has climbed to the top of the tree (or even higher). Life below is still hard-going. The "sodden floor" is muddy (58), and life is a battle to the death between "the boarhound and the boar" – two killers in conflict (59). Various cultures (notably the Picts and Druids) recognized a boar constellation in the sky. From the perspective of the universe, however, life has a "pattern"; it is "reconciled among the stars" (60-61). The cycle of our life and death is connected to the universe. There *is* a pattern, and where there is a pattern, there is *meaning*.

This section is a plea not to get caught up in the minutia of existence. Life brings garlic, which feeds the body, and sapphires, which feed the esthetic sense. There is a context to our existence; it is not arbitrary.

Four Quartets: *Burnt Norton*

Part II, Lines 62 – 89 ("At the still … time is conquered.")

Notes

"At the still point of the turning world" (62) – Deborah Leiter draws a close comparison between *Four Quartets* and *Walden*, "While Eliot would not likely have called himself a Transcendentalist, his quest for the 'still point of the turning world' as expressed in *Four Quartets* could certainly be explained as a semi-mystical quest for Transcendent moments in the real world, in much the same way that *Walden* tells the story of Thoreau's pursuit of the Transcendent moments in the real world" ("Toward the Still Point," 34-35). Leiter continues:

> The orthodox Christian doctrines of the Incarnation, in which God entered human flesh and died in that flesh, then was raised with a touchable body, and the corresponding idea that this enfleshed person of the Trinity will return not to take humans to heaven but to establish a heavenly kingdom on a new earth, when placed as a subtext to Eliot's imagery, reinforces the idea that Eliot's poem affirms not just the timeless or the heavenly but, as the speaker of the poem states, both aspects coming together in the true paradox of the "intersection of the timeless with time" (DS 201-202), of heaven with earth. In fact, Eliot's moments, like Thoreau's (and unlike Emerson's and those of the Eastern scriptures both Eliot and Thoreau referred to in their works), never take one out of the earthly context in which he experienced them. On the contrary, Eliot's accurate descriptions of his real-life still point moments—in his visit to the house of Burnt Norton, at the town of East Coker, on his way across the Atlantic, at a church in the English countryside – reaffirm and give greater richness and understanding to aspects of these earthly surroundings. (Ibid 38)

"*Erhebung*" (74) – The closest synonym is 'elevation.' Hegel used '*Erhebung*' to refer to the fusion of two contradictory ideas.

"To be conscious is not to be in time" (85) – Roger Bellin explains that "this apparently pivotal line can be understood at least three distinct ways. It can mean that a truly mystical consciousness, once attained, allows the mystic an extra-temporal vantage point (this may be the most obvious reading in the context of the whole body of the Quartets). But it can just as well be taken to say that every person's consciousness already contains an element of awareness of the timeless, though it lives inside of the temporality of our lives (this reading is more salient in the context of the preceding lines, 'Time past and time future / Allow but a little consciousness' – this 'little' may be all we can aspire to). Or it can mean that human thought is only possible within time, and so to be conscious is always to die ('not to be, in time'), presaged by the earlier reference to 'heaven and damnation / Which flesh cannot endure'. All of these meanings must be held at once…" ("The Seduction of Argument and the Danger of Parody in the Four Quartets," *Twentieth Century Literature*, vol. 53, no. 4. 2007. Web. Nov.11, 2021)

"arbour" (86) – Arbour (arbor) is an obsolete word for a garden, orchard, or lawn. An arbor may also be a leafy glade or bower shaded by trees, vines, shrubs trained about a trellis.

"smokefall" (87) – A rather archaic term for the close of the day just before nightfall – dusk, twilight.

Commentary

The "still point of the turning world" (62) can only be perceived in the present moment where "past and future are gathered" (65). However, that is difficult because it involves achieving a sense of permanent significance in a modern world that is all about flux and disintegration. The moment of perception of eternity/infinity comes in the midst of human involvement in the temporal world that is a world of flux, locked in the endless movement from past to present to future. It is a seemingly impossible state, being "Neither flesh nor fleshless," so neither human consciousness nor spirit (62) and "neither arrest nor movement" (64). It is the still dance.

The reader might be forgiven for throwing up their hands in despair, but the text is not so impenetrable as it might appear. To perceive a reality and meaning beyond that of human consciousness and the everyday world, humans have to step out of duration (the constant movement of time from one point to the next). Having done this, we can catch a glimpse of the eternal, the infinite, the Godhead (or however we choose to characterize it). We enter a reality that is dynamic but, fairly obviously, is not trapped in progression. Think of a dance – plenty of movement, but the pattern of the dance brings us back to the starting point. Think of the difference between the greatest human music and the music of the spheres.

Deborah Leiter helpfully explains Eliot's imagery:

> The image seems to be like that of the center of the world, or perhaps the sun, which is still itself, in a way, but always rotating the things around it – itself and anything encompassed in its gravity. Thus there is neither "arrest" – because so much is moving around the still point and it is, in a way, the cause of much of the movement – or 'movement' – because the point itself has a stability and a stillness despite the movement around it […] And so the still point is a point at which the confusions of the non-linear (or temporal) journey slip away and a person who has reached a still point can see the true pattern, or "dance," that is taking place around the still point, in the same way that Thoreau could see the pattern of the stars in the stream

or the pattern of the activity around the surface of Walden Pond. From the still point, which in and of itself is not "fixity," one can see the world and its patterns, its interconnections, clearly. (op. cit. 61-62)

The phrase "still point of the turning world" is an oxymoron (62). To state the obvious, the world is going to carry on turning, and chronological time will not stop, but something might be experienced that transcends both – a moment of spiritual stasis. The speaker is describing a paradox, a spiritual experience achieved in a physical world. Thus, it is "[n]either flesh nor fleshless" (62), "[n]either from nor towards," "neither arrest nor movement" (64), "[n]either arrest nor decline" (66). Nor can it be called "fixity" (64) because what we can experience in that moment is nothing if not dynamic, and also because the world is not going to be stopped by it. Notice how much easier it is for the speaker to define what he is talking about by telling us what it is *not*. It is in the timeless that "the dance is" (63), but it is only in the present that the dance can be glimpsed, and there is nothing (of real value) other than the dance.

The symbol of the dance is quite common. Dance is something both in and out of time. Obviously, it takes place in the real world, but for the period of the dance, the real world appears to be suspended, and the dancer gives him/herself entirely to the experience of the dance. It is possible to lose oneself (or perhaps to find oneself) in dancing. Some dances lead to mystical, out-of-body experiences. Think of the Whirling Dervishes, members of a mendicant religious order of Sufi Moslems. As part of their worship, they perform a trance-inducing dance in which the men, who wear billowing white skirts, whirl in circles meant to replicate planets revolving around the sun ("Endangered Phrases" by Steven D. Price). Another example would be the Native American Sioux Sun Dance, in which participants fast and dance for many hours in search of visions.

In his poem "Among School Children" (1926), Irish poet William Butler Yeats (1865-1939) asks:

O chestnut tree, great rooted blossomer,
Are you the leaf, the blossom or the bole?
O body swayed to music, O brightening glance,
How can we know the dancer from the dance?

Is the chestnut tree "the leaf, the blossom or the bole [i.e., the trunk]"? Clearly, it is all three – they cannot be separated. So man is body, mind, and soul – they cannot be separated. Life is a process that involves movement, like the movement of a "body swayed to music." Yeats would say that the dancer momentarily becomes the dance; mind and body are fused. Eliot would add that, while this is true, the dance itself remains after the dancer has moved on, even after the dancer has died. So, for Eliot, in "the still point" discovered in the present moment (62), we experience the beauty of life captured in "the dance" (67). That is, given lasting form, as the landscaper gave the garden at Burnt Norton lasting form – a pattern that the visitor can experience, relive and recreate, and in doing so, experience his own moment of transcendent spirituality.

This is all very abstract. We are being asked to conceive of an oxymoron: an instant in the present that not merely contains past and future but transcends time altogether. This is rather like a person who has conceptualized a square circle trying to explain in geometry class just how such a thing is possible. It might help to step away from the text for a moment to consider accounts of others who have had experiences similar to those the narrator is describing since, self-evidently, he is not describing an experience unique to himself. For this reason, the experiences of others may be instructive.

There are many such accounts in Colin Wilson's 2009 book *Super Consciousness: The Quest for the Peak Experience*. For example, Wilson cites the American philosopher, historian, and psychologist, William James (1842-1910), who in his essay "A Suggestion About Mysticism" (1910) gives an account of four personal experiences:

> which could only be described as very sudden and incomprehensible enlargements of the conscious field, bringing with them a curious sense of cognition of real fact. In each of the three like cases, the experience broke in abruptly upon a perfectly commonplace situation and lasted perhaps less than two minutes [...] What happened each time was that I seemed all at once to be reminded of a past experience; and this reminiscence, ere I could conceive or name it distinctly, developed into something further that belonged with it, this in turn into something further still, and so on, until the process faded out, leaving me amazed at the sudden vision of increasing ranges of distant fact of which I could give no articulate account. The mode of consciousness was perceptual, not conceptual – the field expanding so fast that there seemed no time for conception or identification to get in its work. There was a strongly exciting sense that my knowledge of past (or present?) reality was enlarging pulse by pulse, but so rapidly that my intellectual processes could not keep up the pace. The content was thus entirely lost to retrospection — it sank into the limbo into which dreams vanish as we gradually awake. The feeling – I won't call it belief— that I had had a sudden opening, had seen through a window, as it were, distant realities that incomprehensibly belonged with my own life, was so acute that I can not shake it off to-day. (*The Journal of Philosophy, Psychology and Scientific Methods*, vol. 7, no. 4, Journal of Philosophy, Inc., 1910, 87-88.)

At the start of the essay, James gives his opinion that "states of mystical intuition may be only very sudden and great extensions of the ordinary 'field of consciousness'" (Ibid 85). This is a viewpoint with which Wilson would fully concur since it was his central belief that a person could learn to generate peak experiences at will.

In *New Pathways in Psychology* (1972), Wilson quotes the views of American psychologist Abraham H. Maslow (1908-1970), who revolutionized psychology by studying mentally healthy rather than unhealthy people. In his essay "Lessons from peak experiences" (1962), Maslow explains one significant discovery:

> I found that these individuals tended to report having had something like mystical experiences, moments of the most intense happiness, or even rapture, ecstasy or bliss [...] These were moments of pure, positive happiness, when all doubts, all fears, all inhibitions, all tensions, all weaknesses, were left behind. All separateness from the world disappeared as they felt one with the world, fused with it, really belonging to it, instead of being outside, looking in [...] Perhaps most important of all, however, was the report in these experiences of the feeling that they had really seen the ultimate truth, the essence of things, the secret of life, as if veils had been pulled aside.

True to his scientific approach, Wilson comments, "These experiences are not 'religious' in the ordinary sense. They are natural, and can be studied naturally."

At least so far in his poem, Eliot has given only hints that the kind of experience he is describing might have a spiritual as well as a psychological element. However, his account recalls the response of Austrian neurologist and founder of psychoanalysis Sigmund Freud (1856-1939) in his book *Civilization and Its Discontents* (1929) to a friend's theory about the origins of the religious impulse:

> [The friend wrote that] I had not properly appreciated the ultimate source of religious sentiments. This consists in a peculiar feeling, which never leaves him personally, which he finds shared by many others, and which he may suppose millions more also experience. It is a feeling which he would like to call a sensation of eternity, a feeling as of something limitless, unbounded, something "oceanic." It is, he says, a purely subjective experience, not an article of belief; it implies no assurance of personal immortality, but it is the source of the religious spirit and is taken hold of by the various Churches and religious systems, directed by them into definite channels, and also, no doubt, used up in them. One may rightly call oneself

religious on the ground of this oceanic feeling alone, even
though one reject all beliefs and all illusions. (8)

Freud's reaction to accounts of such experiences is at once very different from
that of Wilson and very similar. Unlike Wilson, who recorded many examples of
peak experiences similar to those described by Freud's friend, Freud denied any
personal experience of them, "I cannot discover this 'oceanic' feeling in myself.
It is not easy to deal scientifically with feelings" (Ibid). Like Freud, however,
Wilson took a scientific view of such feelings and sought to investigate them in
terms of human psychology.

I am frankly not qualified to determine whether the examples cited above are
exactly the same as the experience of past, present, and future time that Eliot's
narrator is describing. To me, they seem very similar, not least in that language
seems inadequate to describe them. One thing, however, is clear: the experience
that Eliot is describing in *Burnt Norton* is the absolute antithesis of that which he
described in *The Waste Land*:

On Margate sands.
I can connect
Nothing with nothing.

I shall bring this brief digression to a close and return to Eliot's text with that
comment.

The narrator attempts to define the experience of the "still point of the turning
world" (62), which is, presumably, what he experienced in the ruined garden
described earlier. It occurred in the present, but it was not, like the present,
involved in duration. The narrator tells us that memory allows him to say *"there*
we have been," but no more than that. He cannot say "where" because, of course,
that place no longer exists, and it was not really a place anyway but a state of
being (68). It is impossible to locate a spiritual state geographically because it
exists outside of space. Nor can he say for "how long, for that would be "to place
it in time" (69). That reminds us that the chronology of a timeline is an illusion:
now gathers together past and future, but the still moment has neither a before
nor an after.

Next, the speaker goes on to define the experience of the "inner freedom" he
felt (70). From what he says, it sounds like the enlightenment that some people
seek through meditation. Mindfulness is being intensely aware of what one is
sensing and feeling in the moment; it is achieving complete awareness of one's
thoughts, emotions, or experiences on a moment-to-moment basis without
feeling the need to interpret or judge. Perhaps, even more, the description
reminds me of accounts of out-of-body experiences where the astral body (or call
it what you will) detaches itself from the physical body and everyday
consciousness. In this state, the spirit is freed from the limitations and constraints
placed upon the physical body, which, of course, can exist only in time.

Experiencing the still point is liberation from "practical desire [...] action and suffering [...] the inner / And the outer compulsion" (71-72). These are all feelings by which man is rendered helpless – the victim of psychological and socio-political forces beyond his ability to control.

In contrast, the experience that the speaker is trying to describe was spiritual or mystical, an instant of "partial ecstasy" (77) surrounded by "a grace of sense," by "a white light [that is] both still and moving" (73). In this state, one achieves liberation from "practical desire" (70) and from both external and internal impulses to do things. This sounds like the Buddhist path to gain release (nibbana/nirvana) from action (kamma/karma) and from its resultant craving ('compulsion') and suffering. The language suggests a Christian benediction that brings the ability to survey life from an elevated position (*"Erhebung"*) without moving, to concentrate without judgment. The experience provides both a "new world / And the old made explicit" (75-76). Above all, this state of "partial ecstacy" (77) offers some degree of "resolution" of the "partial horror" of existence (78). As often in his work, Eliot appears to have in mind Mr. Kurtz's final verdict on human life, "The horror. The horror" (Joseph Conrad, *Heart of Darkness*).

Changing direction, the speaker states that man, whose "changing body" (80) ties him to chronology, is repeatedly called back from the still point by everyday consciousness that is bound to linear time by memories of the past and speculations about the future. It is a form of "enchainment" (79) that is impossible to escape for long because it is essentially a psychological defense mechanism that "[p]rotects" us (81). As our body ages, we become aware of past and future, which are mere diversions from the realization of our mortality. If we face the inevitability of our death, then we must also face "heaven and damnation" (81), but this is the one truth that "flesh cannot endure" (82). It is a terrifying prospect. The human mind does not have the strength to allow such thoughts to become conscious for long. It seeks diversions.

Past and present are, then, a distraction from true consciousness. The heightened consciousness that the narrator has described in the garden is the very opposite of distraction. I think that what Eliot is saying is very much the same as Henry David Thoreau (1817-1862) wrote in *Walden* (1854):

> Not till we are lost, in other words, not till we have lost the
> world, do we begin to find ourselves, and realize where we are
> and *the infinite extent* of our relations. ("The Pond")

For Thoreau, living alone in the woods for two years was the way to put aside the daily trivia of existence and allow his mind to grow through a heightened awareness of present experience, which is both within and outside of time.

The narrator offers a summation. The past and the future "Allow but a little consciousness" because they clutter the mind with things that prevent mindfulness (83). However, consciousness must include facing our mortality and

47

the prospect of our eternal damnation, which is an overwhelming truth. This recalls the warning of the bird that "human kind / Cannot bear very much reality" (42-43). Paradoxically, while consciousness transcends time (bringing together before and after in one supreme moment of heightened awareness), it can only exist within time. Such moments can only be experienced "in the rose-garden […] in the arbour where the rain beat […] in the draughty church at smokefall" (86-87). Such experiences happen "in time" (84), as we are going about our normal day-to-day activities. They become timeless present only as they are recollected in time. In such moments, "time is conquered" (89).

Summary of Part II

The speaker explores the still point, which stands in opposition to the constant movement of chronology. To step out of time is to become conscious of eternity and a truth beyond that of day-to-day existence that gives purpose and meaning to all the events we experience within time. However, for the time-trapped traveler, such insight is challenging, to say the least, because it opens the mind to the reality of "heaven and damnation" (81). That is why we experience true consciousness only in fleeting transcendent moments within time, like the moment in the rose garden. In contrast, our normal consciousness with which we navigate the day-to-day world is really no better than a robot that steers us as we sleepwalk through life.

I cannot improve on Joel Anderson's analysis:

> Time itself, though limiting, nevertheless protects us mortal creatures from both "heaven and damnation." We cannot endure either one in our present, mortal condition. Thus, it is *through time*, and through our use of memory and contemplative recollection of those transcendent moments within time in which we experience the still point, that we are able to *conquer time* and eventually experience full union with the still point. (op. cit.)

Part III, Lines 90 – 113 ("Here is a … this twittering world.")

Notes

"Tumid" (103) – A swollen or enlarged part of the body, or in this case of the mind.
"Eructation" (108) – Belching. In this case, the exhaled breath of these people is like an unhealthy belch.
"torpid" (109) – Inactive, sluggish, apathetic, lethargic.

Commentary

The narrator gives a description of London that recalls the "unreal city" of *The Waste Land*:

Unreal City,
Under the brown fog of a winter dawn,
A crowd flowed over London Bridge, so many,
I had not thought death had undone so many.
Sighs, short and infrequent, were exhaled,
And each man fixed his eyes before his feet.
Flowed up the hill and down King William Street,
To where Saint Mary Woolnoth kept the hours
With a dead sound on the final stroke of nine.
(1. The Burial of the Dead)

Existence in the modern metropolis is a death-in-life; here is existence, not being. It is a place of "disaffection" where people slavishly follow their routines (90). London, notable at this time for its smog (thick fog combined with smoke blocking out the sun), is quintessentially the world of "Time before and time after" where the present is obscured from view (107). More specifically, this section seems to describe a descent into the Underground (perhaps symbolizing Hades), an image for the dark night of the soul. People are scurrying back and forth, too concerned with their day-to-day lives to become conscious in the moment.

This is a world of in-between that can only be described in negative terms. The "dim light" is neither daylight nor darkness (92). This contrasts with the pool in the garden that was "filled with water out of sunlight" and the "light upon the figured leaf" (57) in the tree into which the speaker figuratively rose. The clear light of day would invest "form with lucid stillness / Turning shadow into transient beauty" (93-94), but there is no such light. The turning of the earth made visible in the sun's changing position, and the moving shadows on the ground would suggest some "permanence" by fitting the "lucid stillness" (93) of "transient beauty" (94) into the pattern of days, seasons, and years "suggesting permanence" (95). The speaker here seems to mean the sense of permanence that is conveyed by understanding that the rotation of the earth will continue forever or at least millions of years longer than we live. However, he is also referring to the permanence that comes with a moment of insight that one will remember for the rest of one's life. Similarly, this day-to-day world lacks true darkness – there is never darkness in a city. Sensory deprivation would "purify the soul" (96) by "Cleansing affection for the temporal" (98) – a sort of spiritual detoxification. Thus, here there is no chance for individuals to free themselves from their obsessive dedication to the day-to-day. Sadly, the modern urban world provides "Neither plenitude nor vacancy" (99). People are trapped in non-being.

At the risk of repeating myself, what Eliot is describing as lacking here is what Colin Wilson called 'peak experience' – a moment when the mind escapes from 'the robot' that normally controls our consciousness. Robotic consciousness makes us very good at performing routine functions without thinking (driving the car, making a meal, getting on the underground to go to work, etc.), but the downside is that it leads to a fundamentally passive attitude that takes the world as-it-is to be a given (i.e., *all* there is). As Philip Coultard explains, "Flat, passive consciousness merely reflects it's [sic] outer environment, dimly: [while] 'super consciousness' can illuminate and essentially change the meaning of that supposedly 'outer' environment" ("Super Consciousness 2019"). Wilson argues for a positive philosophic vision "that is based upon a sense of immense meaning, meaning stretching to infinity – a meaning that would exist even if there were no human beings there to see it. It is what saints mean when they speak of God " (*The Angry Years*, 212). Creative vision, a sudden consciousness of what is already there (though usually unseen) in life, produces a state of extreme happiness and optimism. We achieve what Wilson termed cosmic consciousness. The most obvious example from modern literature is Proust's *Swann's Way* when the accidental experience of a cake dipped in tea triggers a moment when "Marcel had ceased to be mediocre, accidental or mortal and had remembered with full clarity the reality of other times and places" (Ibid). This helps to explain what Eliot is describing here as being absent.

Implicitly, Eliot is contrasting the moment of harmony achieved in the rose garden with "the lassitude, boredom, and empty despair of the desperate" souls going about their business in London (Longenecker, "Listening to 'Burnt Norton,'" The Imaginative Conservative, Aug. 24, 2019). These lost souls are "distracted from distraction by distraction" (101). They have "strained time-ridden faces" (99) because they are unable to connect time past and time future in time present. Their minds are dominated by trivia so that they have no more consciousness nor agency than the "bits of paper" that are blown hither and thither in the street by the wind (104). Their thoughts are mere "fancies empty of meaning" (102), resulting in "apathy with no concentration" (103). The reference to paper suggests the occupation of these men (and given the period, they are all men): they are bureaucrats and pen-pushers who deal with bits of paper rather than reality and read about life in their newspapers which they then discard. Paper, in the form of newspapers, schedules, receipts, bills, notes, etc., also suggests a life trapped in time. These people lack agency and do not even seem to be breathing; rather, the wind forces itself "in and out of unwholesome lungs" (106), an image that suggests an unconscious patient on a respirator.

The wind will outlive them since it "blows before and after time" (105), but this is the only way their lives connect with "Time before and time after" (107), and this wind drives them, as it drives paper. Their "unhealthy souls" (108) come out of their mouths like a belch and disappear into "the faded air" instead of rising to heaven (109). Having taken the reader into the Underground, the narrator assures us that life is exactly the same atop "the gloomy hills of London" (110). This is the "twittering world" (113) of the inessential, the ephemeral, transitory and meaningless, and these "unhealthy souls" are imprisoned in it. The word "twittering" (113) contrasts with the meaningful call of the bird in the garden, which earlier led the narrator back to a memory that connected time present and time past in a still moment.

Part III, Lines 114 – 126 ("Descend lower ... and time future.")

Notes

"Descend lower" (114): "In this Underground scene curiously enough, the instructed reader may catch a glimpse of the author, sauntering through the crowd as Alfred Hitchcock does in each of his films. For its locale, Eliot noted, sharing a private joke with his brother in Massachusetts, is specifically the Gloucester Road Station, near the poet's South Kensington headquarters, the point of intersection of the Circle Line with the Piccadilly tube to Russell Square. Whoever would leave the endless circle and entrain for the offices of Faber & Faber must 'descend lower', and by spiral stairs if he chooses to walk. 'This is the one way, and the other is the same'; the other, adjacent to the stairs, is a lift, which he negotiates 'not in movement, but abstention from movement'. As Julia Shuttlethwaite observes in *The Cocktail Party,* 'In a lift I can meditate'." (Hugh Kenner, *The Invisible Poet: T.S. Eliot.* W.H. Allen & Co., 1959.)

"deprivation / And destitution of all property" (117-118) – Relinquishing. It is the same idea that Jesus had as recorded in *Matthew* 19:16-22:

> And, behold, one came and said unto him, Good Master, what good thing shall I do, that I may have eternal life? And he said unto him, Why callest thou me good? there is none good but one, that is, God: but if thou wilt enter into life, keep the commandments. He saith unto him, Which? Jesus said, Thou shalt do no murder, Thou shalt not commit adultery, Thou shalt not steal, Thou shalt not bear false witness, Honour thy father and thy mother: and, Thou shalt love thy neighbour as thyself. The young man saith unto him, All these things have I kept from my youth up: what lack I yet? Jesus said unto him, *If thou wilt be perfect, go and sell that thou hast, and give to the poor, and thou shalt have treasure in heaven: and come and follow me. But when the young man heard that saying, he went away sorrowful: for he had great possessions.* (KJV)

"Desiccation" (119) – Drying out. Effectively killing sensual input.

"Evacuation" (120) – Emptying out (e.g., evacuating the bowels) and, in this case, emptying the mind.

"Inoperancy" (121) – Not functioning effectively.

"In appetency" (125) – A fixed and strong natural desire or craving; an eager appetite. It is the instinctive preference or determined tendency that all animals show to perform certain actions (e.g., birds building nests in spring, salmon swimming upriver to spawn, etc.).

Commentary

Two responses to the human predicament are suggested. The first is to "Descend lower" into "the world of perpetual solitude" (114-115). This seems to involve withdrawing into the self, cutting off all contact with the external world, emptying the mind, and losing both one's social and personal self. Free from the material world in our own "Internal darkness" (117), we can experience the liberating effect of "destitution of all property" (113). The description of the process sounds like instructions for meditation by abandoning the worlds of "sense ... fancy ... [and] spirit" (119-121). I have never been in one, but this sounds like entering an isolation tank. Wikipedia says a "sensory deprivation tank, float tank, float pod, float cabin, flotation tank, or sensory attenuation tank is a pitch-black, light-proof, soundproof environment heated to the same temperature as the skin." The second response appears to be the same because it also involves getting off the merry-go-round of life and being still, but it seems to achieve this by an effort of the mind. Although Eliot would probably be horrified, this sounds like the mantra of the 1960s counter-culture, "Turn on, tune in, drop out." Perhaps less controversially, we talk about opting out of the rat race of modern life. The key is in "abstention from movement" (124), inhabiting the still point of the turning world, abstaining from movement. In contrast, the external world continues to move around us with the people in it operating on 'automatic pilot,' the robotic consciousness that helps us navigate our day-to-day existence. I have this visual image of someone standing at the center of a carousel watching the riders go round and round. Of the two, the second seems the more accurate description of what the speaker experienced in the rose garden.

The image of the world moving "on its metalled ways / Of time past and time future" calls to mind locomotives running on rails (125-126). Perhaps Eliot had in mind the ubiquitous London Underground. This, in turn, suggests timetables, because trains have to run on time. The people are like the trains, dominated by "time past and time future" (126) with no time in their busy lives for time present. The phrase "metalled ways" also conveys inflexibility. The world is predictable, regimented. This suggests the quotation often erroneously attributed to Albert Einstein (1879-1955), "The definition of insanity is doing the same thing over and over again but expecting different results." Whoever said it, that seems to nail the insanity of the rut that is modern life.

Summary of Part III

Here the narrator explores the spiritual discipline necessary to rise above man's emersion in the trivial world of society. The distracting world must be put aside, as must the individual self, the individual ego or personality that we have developed to live in the world. Only then is one ready for spiritual illumination.

Part IV, Lines 127 – 135 ("Time and the ... the turning world.")

Notes

"Time and the bell" (127) – Inevitably, one thinks of John Donne's famous sermon:

> PERCHANCE he for whom this bell tolls may be so ill, as that he knows not it tolls for him; and perchance I may think myself so much better than I am, as that they who are about me, and see my state, may have caused it to toll for me, and I know not that. The church is Catholic, universal, so are all her actions; all that she does belongs to all. [...] when she buries a man, that action concerns me: all mankind is of one author, and is one volume; when one man dies, one chapter is not torn out of the book, but translated into a better language; and every chapter must be so translated; God employs several translators; some pieces are translated by age, some by sickness, some by war, some by justice; but God's hand is in every translation, and his hand shall bind up all our scattered leaves again for that library where every book shall lie open to one another. [...] The bell doth toll for him that thinks it doth; and though it intermit again, yet from that minute that that occasion wrought upon him, he is united to God. [...] Who bends not his ear to any bell which upon any occasion rings? but who can remove it from that bell which is passing a piece of himself out of this world?
>
> No man is an island, entire of itself; every man is a piece of the continent, a part of the main. If a clod be washed away by the sea, Europe is the less, as well as if a promontory were, as well as if a manor of thy friend's or of thine own were: *any man's death diminishes me, because I am involved in mankind, and therefore never send to know for whom the bells tolls; it tolls for thee.* [...]

The words also recall "Elegy Written in a Country Churchyard" (1751) by Thomas Gray (1716-1771):

> The *curfew tolls the knell of parting day*;
> The lowing herd wind slowly o'er the lea;
> The ploughman homeward plods his weary way,
> And leaves the world to darkness and to me.

"the kingfisher's wing" (133) – This reference brings to mind the poem "As Kingfishers Catch Fire" By Gerard Manley Hopkins (1844-1889):

> As kingfishers catch fire, dragonflies draw flame;
> As tumbled over rim in roundy wells

Stones ring; like each tucked string tells, each hung bell's
Bow swung finds tongue to fling out broad its name;
Each mortal thing does one thing and the same:
Deals out that being indoors each one dwells;
Selves – goes itself; *myself* it speaks and spells,
Crying *Whát I dó is me: for that I came.*

I say móre: the just man justices;
Keeps grace: thát keeps all his goings graces;
Acts in God's eye what in God's eye he is –
Christ – for Christ plays in ten thousand places,
Lovely in limbs, and lovely in eyes not his
To the Father through the features of men's faces.

Professor Lynn Cohen explains the significance of the kingfisher symbol in Hopkins's poem, "[It] represents, paradoxically, both mortality and immortality. The iridescent plumage of the spectacular kingfisher begins as a symbol of robust and fiery life: 'As kingfishers catch fire, dragonflies dráw flame.' It moves to the death tolling warning, 'Each mortal thing does one thing and the same.'" For Eliot, as for Hopkins, Christ, like the kingfisher that symbolizes Him, is the only uniter of opposites, especially the ultimate opposites of mortality and immortality. Nicholas Kotar captures Eliot's meaning perfectly, "Truth is an experience of transcendent reality that leaves you with no doubt of its presence, but that you can't find until you experience it directly. Truth is not an idea. Truth, as we Christians know, is a Person. Like the kingfisher, truth is found in the "still, small voice" (*1 Kingdoms* 19:12) that can only be encountered with humility, patience, and many thousand attempts at perfection" ("The Kingfisher as a Symbol for Culture Creation in Crisis," Sep. 15, 2020. Web. Nov. 13, 2021).
"the still point" (135) – Compare Thomas Merton (1915-1968), *The Way of Chuang Tzu* (1965):

> Tao is obscured when men understand only one pair of opposites,
> or concentrate only on a partial aspect of being.
> Then clear expression also becomes muddled by mere wordplay,
> affirming this one aspect and denying all the rest.
>
> The pivot of Tao passes through the center
> where all affirmations and denials converge.
> He who grasps the pivot is *at the still-point*
> from which all movements and oppositions
> can be seen in their right relationship [...]
>
> Abandoning all thought of imposing a limit or taking sides,
> he rests in direct intuition.

Four Quartets: *Burnt Norton*

Commentary

It is night, "Time and the bell have buried the day" (127). The bell may be a curfew bell or perhaps a bell that tolls for a funeral, in which case night is a metaphor for death. Students are familiar with the bells that mark the beginning and end of classes, and Schmoop reminds me that the New York Stock Exchange uses a bell to mark the start and end of trading each day. The speaker is saying that our modern way of life has pretty much buried us under a mound of trivia: "Time and the bell" tie us into the world of duration. The passing bell that marks our death will 'liberate' us from linear time, but what will succeed it? The "black cloud" of the night "carries the sun away" (127) is a violent abduction image that suggests both the irresistible onward movement of chronological time and also the absolute difference between life (light) and death (the complete absence of light).

The narrator then asks rhetorically whether the sunflower, clematis, or yew tree will "turn to us [...] Stray down, bend to us [...] Clutch and cling" (129-131). The questions begin innocently enough, but the alliteration of the words 'clutch,' 'cling,' 'chill,' and 'curled' produces an increasingly urgent tone. It seems that we are dead and buried and that flowers and trees reach down through the earth to find us. The personification of the yew (its roots are "fingers") is also urgent. The yew has long associations with English graveyards. From Druid times, it has been associated with age and rebirth because as the original tree dies, new growth emerges. Thus, the roots reaching down to each corpse buried in the graveyard symbolize rebirth, with the spirit reborn in the same way the tree regenerates. The speaker is asking whether that which is eternal will reach down to mortal man. The possibility that it might has been prompted by his experience of a moment out of time yet within time in the garden at Burnt Norton – a spiritual experience that has stayed with the narrator.

The narrator is presenting the death of the day as a symbol for the man's mortality and thus of the unstoppable rush of time. In death, we become part of the natural world, which is why the plants reach down to our bodies under the ground. The yew is a pagan symbol of rebirth that suggests the promise of Christian resurrection. Matthiessen states:

> [T]he chief contrast around which Eliot constructs this poem is that between the view of time as a mere continuum, and the difficult paradoxical Christian view of how man lives both "in and out of time," how he is immersed in the flux and yet can penetrate to the eternal by apprehending timeless existence within time and above it. (183).

This at least offers some prospect of resurrection. Perhaps death is not the end we conceive it to be.

In the day (i.e., life), the bright colors of the kingfisher's wings reflect the sunlight and move on. However, the reflected light remains "silent ... [and] still,"

55

presumably in the mind of the observer (130). It exists at "the still point of the turning world" (135), where the present that is always now and now contains past, present, and future because chronology has no existence.

Schmoop suggests that the kingfisher may be a punning reference to the British myth of the fisher king to which Eliot refers in *The Waste Land*. The fisher king is "a traditional symbol of something that can bring back fertility to our barren modern landscape and restore our souls to their former glory." This clearly fits into the theme of rebirth in this section. However, it is even more on point to see the kingfisher as symbolic of Christ, the man-god who existed both within and outside time.

Summary of Part IV

At death, we return to the soil and fit into the pattern of generation, birth, and death, the life cycle in the physical world. However, the bell that signals the ending of the day (and eventually of our life) also calls us to pray. The yew trees in graveyards symbolize both death and resurrection. The speaker then explores the paradox that we will fully comprehend the pattern that gives our existence meaning at the point of death. In the stillness of death, we experience the still point of eternity through faith in Jesus Christ. As we read in *Revelation* 1:18, "*I am* he that liveth, and was dead; and, behold, I am alive for evermore, Amen; and have the keys of hell and of death" (KJV).

Part V, Lines 136 – 157 ("Words move … the disconsolate chimera.")

Notes

"a Chinese jar" (141) – This is another version of the urn in "Ode on a Grecian Urn" (1819) by the English Romantic poet John Keats (1795-1821). The Chinese jar represents the capacity of art to transcend the limitations of the moment, to achieve a kind of victory over, or different perspective on, time. In its physical existence, which embodies form and pattern, the jar can overcome the usual imprecision of human expression. Eliot suggests that poetry, which takes advantage of linguistic form and pattern, may also achieve transcendence.

"the stillness of the violin, while the note lasts" (143) – In *The Timeless Moment* (1946), the writer Warner Allen (1918-1978) describes a perception he had during a classical concert that makes this distinction perfectly. Allen's account is particularly important since he actually refers to it as an instance of "what Mr. T. S. Eliot calls 'the intersection of the timeless moment.'" *The Timeless Moment* was published by Eliot's firm Faber and Faber.

> When the writer was on the threshold of fifty, it occurred to him, as it must have occurred to many another ordinary journalist, no less hostile to the apparent sloppiness of fashionable mysticism than he was, that he had lived for nearly half a century without discerning in life any pattern or rational

purpose. His views on the matter might have been roughly summed up in a vague notion that the meaning of the universe was shrouded in impenetrable darkness by the Powers of Life and Death, for fear that life should lose its savour as a brave adventure, if the mystery of death and suffering was solved and uncertainty was exchanged for the assurance of future beatitude.

A curiously vivid dream shook his faith in this tentative explanation of human ignorance, though he could not possibly have said what the appearance in his sleep of a light brighter than the sun had to do with the matter.

Almost before he knew it, *he found himself involved in the task of recalling everything he could remember of his past life in the hope of tracing some pattern and design that underlay its outward incoherence and fitting the disjointed episodes of his thoughts, feelings and actions into the unity of a rational purpose*. This quest of truth led through paths of unforeseen darkness and danger, but within a year of clock-time an answer came.

It flashed up lightning-wise during a performance of Beethoven's Seventh Symphony at the Queen's Hall, in that triumphant fast movement when 'the morning stars sang together and all the sons of God shouted for joy'. The swiftly flowing continuity of the music was not interrupted, so that *what Mr. T. S. Eliot calls 'the intersection of the timeless moment' must have slipped into the interval between two demi-semi-quavers*. 'When, long after, I analysed the happening in the cold light of retrospect, it seemed to fall into three parts:

– first the mysterious event itself which occurred in an infinitesimal fraction of a split second; this I learned afterwards from Santa Teresa to call *Union with God*;

– then Illumination, a wordless stream of complex feelings in which the experience of Union combined with the rhythmic emotion of the music like a sunbeam striking with iridescence the spray above a waterfall – a stream that was continually swollen by tributaries of associated Experience;

– lastly Enlightenment, the recollection in tranquillity of the whole complex of Experience as it were embalmed in thought-forms and words.

Since words are the only currency in which a writer can deal, it might seem impossible for him to go outside the third stage of the Vision, when the simplicity of the original event amalgamated with other Experience has been measured and divided by thought and language into the arbitrary sections defined by words. *Memory, however, preserves not only the final representation in its clear-cut shape, but also the more or less shadowy traces of the process which led to it.*

However one decides to explain the experience that Allen had (religious ecstasy, enlightenment, etc.), it is clear that for the first time, he experienced enhanced or heightened perception in which music had a meaning beyond the pleasure of listening to the notes.

"The Word in the desert / Is most attacked by voices of temptation" (154-155) – For the identification of Christ with the Word, see *John* 1:1-14:

> In the beginning was the Word, and *the Word was with God, and the Word was God.* The same was in the beginning with God. All things were made by him; and without him was not any thing made that was made. In him was life; and the life was the light of men. And the light shineth in darkness; and the darkness comprehended it not. There was a man sent from God, whose name was John. The same came for a witness, to bear witness of the Light, that all men through him might believe. He was not that Light, but was sent to bear witness of that Light. That was the true Light, which lighteth every man that cometh into the world. He was in the world, and the world was made by him, and the world knew him not. He came unto his own, and his own received him not. But as many as received him, to them gave he power to become the sons of God, even to them that believe on his name: Which were born, not of blood, nor of the will of the flesh, nor of the will of man, but of God. And *the Word was made flesh, and dwelt among us,* (and we beheld his glory, the glory as of the only begotten of the Father,) full of grace and truth. (KJV)

For Christ in the desert, see *Matthew* 4.1-11:

> Then was Jesus led up of the Spirit into the wilderness to be tempted of the devil. And when he had fasted forty days and forty nights, he was afterward an hungred. And when the tempter came to him, he said, If thou be the Son of God, command that these stones be made bread. But he answered and said, It is written, Man shall not live by bread alone, but by every word that proceedeth out of the mouth of God. Then the devil taketh him up into the holy city, and setteth him on a pinnacle of the temple, and saith unto him, If thou be the Son of God, cast thyself down: for it is written, He shall give his

angels charge concerning thee: And in their hands they shall bear thee up, Lest at any time thou dash thy foot against a stone. Jesus said unto him, It is written again, Thou shalt not tempt the Lord thy God. Again, the devil taketh him up into an exceeding high mountain, and sheweth him all the kingdoms of the world, and the glory of them; and saith unto him, All these things will I give thee, if thou wilt fall down and worship me. Then saith Jesus unto him, Get thee hence, Satan: for it is written, Thou shalt worship the Lord thy God, and him only shalt thou serve. Then the devil leaveth him, and, behold, angels came and ministered unto him. (KJV)

"chimera" (157) –In Greek mythology, the Chimera was a fire-breathing monster usually depicted in art with a lion's head, goat's body, and serpent's tail. In biology, chimeras are animals composed of cells that originate from two (or more) different species. The word is used of any grotesque monster having disparate parts.

Commentary

The narrator turns his attention to art. Words and music move "[o]nly in time" (137) – a poem or a symphony takes a certain amount of time to write, edit, publish, distribute, read or perform, and experience. Words and musical notes are time-dependent, locked into what Warner Allen calls "clock-time." But if that is all they are then they have a short 'shelf-life.' Once spoken, words "reach / Into the silence" (138-139). They literally disappear, and the same may be said of musical notes.

As we read a poem or listen to a symphony, the clock of our lives keeps ticking. A play by Shakespeare and a symphony by Beethoven are finite performances, and in this, they resemble humans because "that which is only living / Can only die" (137-138). This puts me in mind of works of literature or music that were immediately popular but quickly disappeared without a trace – the blockbuster bestsellers that were soon out of print and the one-hit-wonders who topped the charts with one song and were never heard of again.

This fatalistic view of the pointlessness of life sounds reminiscent of Macbeth's thoughts when he has understood the emptiness of the life that he has gained through regicide:

> Tomorrow, and tomorrow, and tomorrow,
> Creeps in this petty pace from day to day,
> To the last syllable of recorded time;
> And all our yesterdays have lighted fools
> The way to dusty death. Out, out, brief candle!
> Life's but a walking shadow, a poor player,
> That struts and frets his hour upon the stage,

And then is heard no more. It is a tale
Told by an idiot, full of sound and fury,
Signifying nothing.
(Shakespeare, *Macbeth*, Act 5 Scene 5)

However, words and musical notes can escape the tyranny of chronology. By their form and pattern, and only by their form and pattern, words and musical notes can reach the "stillness" (141). At this point, the reader remembers the "formal pattern" of the garden at Burnt Norton still discernable after centuries (31). As an example of what he means, the narrator cites "a Chinese jar" (141) – a delicate ceramic, painted presumably with rural scenes, that exists both in time as an artifact and out of time as a timeless representation of a moment in time. Thus poetry, music, and the ceramic each "[m]oves perpetually in its stillness" (142). That is, each exists in chronological time but is unchanged by chronology. John Keats' "Ode to a Grecian Urn" makes the same point. The action presented on the urn is dynamic: its stillness marks the "coexistence" of present and past and future (140).

This is all pretty mystical stuff, and the narrator struggles to communicate what he means. We all recognize "the stillness of the violin, while the note lasts" (143), but that is not it. Although it can *seem* endless, that kind of stillness will soon come to an end. At most, the movement of time has *appeared* to be suspended for an instant. However, the Chinese jar, a poem, or a quartet achieve "the co-existence" of time and timelessness (144). That is, they are both simultaneously inside and outside of time, just like the dance, though the speaker does not make the connection. Their very being triumphs over time, bringing all time into a still *now*:

> Or say that the end precedes the beginning,
> And the end and the beginning were always there
> Before the beginning and after the end.
> And all is always now. (145-148)

We are so used to thinking in chronological terms of a beginning, a middle, and an end that we tend to assume that is the only way to define time. However, when we read a poem by Keats or listen to a symphony by Beethoven or look at an ancient Japanese ceramic, chronological time no longer exists. We are back to the moment in which they were made. Suddenly we realize that linear time, far from being the only form is time, is an illusion experienced only by human beings on earth. God does not exist in chronology, clock-time, duration, or whatever else one wants to call it.

The idea of the co-existence of past and future in the present recalls the poem's opening but in a much more positive way. There, the possibilities seemed to be unreal, and the choice they seemed to offer being illusory and existing only in abstraction. The very real experience that the narrator had in the garden changed his view about that. Here, the alternative to be trapped in time is not a fleeting flight into 'what-if' but the identification of a pattern linking past and future, enabling us to "reach / The stillness" (140-141) to apprehend truth. I am reminded of the caddie Bagger Vance in Stephen Pressfield's novel *The Legend of Bagger Vance* (1995) when he is trying to explain to Captain Junah how to find his lost golf swing, which, he says, exists "somewhere in the harmony of all that is, all that was, all that will be." Throughout the novel, golf is used as a metaphor for life. Later, Vance asserts that to play the perfect golf shot, you have to "See the place where the tides and the seasons and the turning of the earth all come together. Where everything that is, becomes one." (These quotations are from the movie version of this modern variation on the Sanskrit poem *The Bhagavad Gita*.)

If the secret to timeless beauty is form and pattern in art, it follows that these are difficult to achieve. The speaker gives a description that any writer will recognize of the difficult process of composition and the obstinate refusal of words to make a meaningful pattern because they "slip, slide, perish, / Decay with imprecision" (150-151). I feel that way right now as I struggle to get down on paper the ideas suggested by Eliot's poem. Words are so often used in the world for "[s]hrieking ... / Scolding, mocking, or merely chattering" (152-153) that they are unused to being disciplined to order and pattern. Language has been degraded by casual use. Deborah Leiter comments:

> This passage shows the speaker's awareness that words, unlike the Chinese jar that manages to become a still point of the turning world just before this passage, have difficulty achieving "still point"-ness – in other words, becoming true, unbroken intersections of God with humanity, or in still other words, achieving scriptural status. (56)

The last four lines of this section draw a religious analogy. "The Word in the desert" (note the capitalization) recalls the beginning of the *Gospel of John,* which refers to Christ as the Word, "In the beginning was the Word, and the Word was with God, and the Word was God" (1:1, KJV). The incarnation of Christ, the Son of God embodied in flesh or the taking on of human form, means that He *became* the still moment, – since Christ is both in time (c.4 BCE to c.30 CE) and eternal. Also referenced is the story of Christ going into the desert for forty days and forty nights where Satan tempted him (see Notes above). This explains the Word being "attacked by voices of temptation," in the desert. The great truth of personal salvation that Jesus came to earth to offer was attacked not only by the temptation to give up his message but is negated by, "The crying shadow in the funeral dance, / The loud lament of the disconsolate chimera" (154-155). The temptation is to allow the shadow of death to dissuade us from attempting to achieve something in art or faith that will stand both inside and outside of time. Man is like the "chimera" since he is both mortal and (potentially) immortal. It is an uncomfortable position to contemplate, let alone to maintain, which explains the adjective "disconsolate" (157).

Defeatism, nihilism, the conviction that life had no meaning because God is dead, the existentialism of Sartre and Camus that was just becoming fashionable at the time Eliot wrote – these are the enemies of achieving peace by perceiving the moment that is both inside and outside of time. These are the enemies of producing art that is simultaneously temporal and eternal, of the world and yet outside the world, dynamic but still.

Part V, Lines 158 – 174 ("The detail of … before and after.")

Notes

"the figure of the ten stairs" (159) – The phrase 'dark night of the soul' signifies a spiritual crisis on the journey toward union with God. Although such a crisis is usually of short duration, it can last for years. *The Dark Night of the Soul* by St. John of the Cross (1542-1591) states that "there are ten steps on the mystical ladder of divine love." The first five stairs involve renunciation and descent; the second five stairs involve fulfillment and ascent to unity.

Commentary

This section reads increasingly like riddles, but the difficulties are more apparent than real.

The "figure of the ten stairs" (159) refers to the principle metaphor of spiritual ascent of St. John of the Cross. What exactly is movement? Climbing or descending the stairs is movement, and so is the artistic representation of a person climbing stairs. "The detail of the pattern is movement" (158) refers both to the written word, music, and ceramics. On the Chinese vase, the painted scenes appear to be dynamic. Similarly, the pattern in the formal garden around which the narrator and his companion walked is dynamic.

In this section, the speaker is distinguishing between two different types of movement: movement in the world and movement in eternity. Desire is an internal, psychological movement that leads to an external movement; as such, it is not "in itself [i.e., inherently or necessarily] desirable" (161). "Love is itself unmoving" (162) because love simply *is*. However, the origin of love is in movement, and love is also the cause of future movement because it impacts the way people interact. I think the narrator is saying that if love, which is essentially "Timeless, and undesiring" (164), can only express itself in the external world, it is "Caught in the form of limitation" (166), that is chronology – time before and time after. Thus, to feel love is to be trapped between "unbeing [earthly love] and being [divine love]" (167). To be in two worlds at once (as a work of art also is) is to be neither fully one thing nor the other.

Abruptly, the narrator returns to the real world. The 's' alliteration conveys the abrupt penetration of a "shaft of sunlight" illuminating the motes in the air

(168). I can relate to this. I remember being in the hall of a medieval manor in England forty years ago when I noticed beams of light streaming through a stained-glass window illuminating the motes that floated and danced in the air. Quite spontaneously, I was having a peak experience in which everything in the world appeared suddenly to make sense and to be surpassingly beautiful. That experience (which lasted for perhaps four minutes) has never left me. I can reenter it at will; sometimes, I reenter it spontaneously.

In this case, the "shaft of sunlight" appears to be a moment of inspiration, a reminder from the natural world of the beauty of life precisely like the sunlight that seemed to fill the pool at Burnt Norton with water. The sunlight cuts through the dust to awaken the sound of laughter from the children hidden in the foliage. This is a reference back to "The unheard music in the shrubbery" (27), where "the leaves were full of children" (40). It has been suggested that the laughter may be mocking the narrator as the children draw him into speculation and memory. However, I do not get that impression. Instead, this appears to be a genuine call to experience a perfect moment in time that takes the narrator out of time, and the speaker calls on the reader to appreciate it, "Quick now, here, now, always –" (172). That line, in turn, echoes the message of the bird, "Quick ... find them, find them" (19). Not to follow the invitation would be to waste the potential moment, which is what people so often do because they are so focused on "the waste sad time / Stretching before and after" (173-174). That is, the chronological timeline of their lives so confines people that they do not take the time to stop and contemplate a reality and meaning beyond mortality. Thus, the poem ends on a very affirmative note.

An anonymous annotation of the text helpfully explains, "The co-existence of past and future recalls the opening of the poem, but the earlier bleakness – where possibilities are unreal and so choice illusory – gives way to a more consoling view. The pattern linking past and future is what enables us to "reach the stillness", to apprehend truth despite the slipperiness of words" (genius.com). Within our ordinary lives, we occasionally experience the still point. This is a glimpse of a reality beyond the time-bound world. These moments of perception come and quickly go, but they leave us with a feeling of the waste that life seems to be in comparison to the ecstatic perception of the still point.

Summary of Part V

The speaker explores the limits of language. Again, he explores a paradox: we need words to understand the still point, but words cannot describe something that can only be experienced. Christ, the Word in the desert, was tempted by Satan's words to test God. In the same way, man's spiritual faith and aspirations are "attacked" by the temptations of the material world (155). Thus, desire is a distracting internal (i.e., psychological) movement that leads to undesirable actions in time. Human love is similarly "the cause and end of movement" (163) when it is trapped "in the aspect of time" (165). In contrast, true love (i.e., divine love) is timeless and unmoving because it asks nothing.

The most obvious way to escape one's entrapment in the everyday world of chronology and linear time is through memory. The experience of a vivid memory, which may last only for seconds and at the most for minutes, obviously occurs in time, but the experience itself takes one out of time. It creates a perception of immortality, meaning, and happiness that we simply do not feel in our everyday lives. Proust explains the essence of such experiences when he says that he experienced past events "at the present moment and at the same time in the context of a distant moment, so that the past was made to encroach upon the present and I was made to doubt whether I was in the one or the other." In such peak experiences, mono-consciousness, which is our normal experience of life, is temporarily replaced by duo-consciousness (i.e., we feel ourselves to be in two places at the same time) and the joy we feel is "the recognition that consciousness if not restricted to the boring down-to-earth present in which we are all stuck for most of our lives" (Wilson, *Beyond the Occult*, 114). What we experience is what G. K. Chesterton called "absurd good news."

EAST COKER (1940)

Preparing to Read

Time for some more mental stretches to prepare for the second quartet.

1. What or where do you consider your beginning to be? There are many ways of interpreting that question (historical, psychological, spiritual, etc.) and probably several answers for each way of interpreting it. Make a list of possible answers. Which do you consider the most satisfactory?

2. Going back as far as you have knowledge, from where does your family originate? If it is a distant town (perhaps in another country), have you ever made the 'pilgrimage' to find your roots? What was it like?

3. Is there a particular place associated with the history of your family that you have not visited and really would like to? What is the particular attraction of this place?

4. Have you ever been in a building, town, or location that was once important to a member of your family? How did the place make you feel?

5. What or where do you consider will be your end? There are many ways of interpreting that question (historical, psychological, spiritual, etc.) and probably several answers for each way of interpreting it. Make a list of possible answers. Which do you consider the most satisfactory?

Part I, Lines 1 – 13 "In my beginning … a silent motto.")

Notes

"In my beginning is my end" (1) – This recalls the *ouroboros* (or *uroboros*), one of the oldest mystical symbols in the world depicting a serpent or dragon eating its own tail. It is first found in Egypt c.1600 BCE. The *ouroboros* is often interpreted as a symbol for eternal cyclic renewal or the cycle of life, death, and rebirth. As a gnostic and alchemical symbol, the ouroboros "expresses the unity of all things, material and spiritual, which never disappear but perpetually change form in an eternal cycle of destruction and re-creation" (*Britannica*). To Gnostics, the cyclic nature of the serpent symbolizes the concepts of salvation and eternity.

"And a time" (10 & 11) – The narrator echoes the Bible, in this case, *Ecclesiastes* 3:1-8:

> *To every thing there is a season, and a time to every purpose under the heaven*: A time to be born, and a time to die; a time to plant, and a time to pluck up that which is planted; A time to kill, and a time to heal; a time to break down, and a time to build up; A time to weep, and a time to laugh; a time to mourn, and a

time to dance; A time to cast away stones, and a time to gather stones together; a time to embrace, and a time to refrain from embracing; A time to get, and a time to lose; a time to keep, and a time to cast away; A time to rend, and a time to sew; a time to keep silence, and a time to speak; A time to love, and a time to hate; a time of war, and a time of peace. (KJV)

Commentary

The narrator continues to speculate on the theme of time. Fortunately for the reader, he does so in a much more concrete and accessible way. "In my beginning is my end," he says (1). That is true in the obvious sense that humans are mortal. From the moment that a human emerges from not-consciousness (whatever that state actually *is*) into consciousness (i.e., is born), they will inevitably die and return to not-consciousness. We do not understand this from the moment of our birth, but most children have a realistic understanding of death before they are nine. (Interestingly, it is such a shock that hardly anyone can remember the moment the mortality penny dropped, even people who can remember their first ice cream or their first bike). Once again, it would be churlish to ignore the author's biography. East Coker was home to his ancestors, and in this sense, the village represents his beginning; near the end of his life, he has returned. (Eliot would live another twenty years. At what date Eliot determined that his remains would lie in the parish church, I do not know.)

The opening statement recalls *Job* 14:1-2: "Man that is born of a woman is of few days and full of trouble. He cometh forth like a flower, and is cut down: he fleeth also as a shadow, and continueth not" (KJV). It also seems to parallel the Church of England Order for the Burial of the Dead. This includes the statement, "Forasmuch as it hath pleased Almighty God of his great mercy to take unto himself the soul of our dear brother here departed: we therefore commit his body to the ground; *earth to earth, ashes to ashes, dust to dust.*" I am also put in mind of poem XXXII from *A Shropshire Lad* (1896) by the English poet A. E. Housman (1859-1936):

> From far, from eve and morning
>   And yon twelve-winded sky,
> The stuff of life to knit me
>   Blew hither: here am I.
> *Now – for a breath I tarry*
>   *Nor yet disperse apart –*
> Take my hand quick and tell me,
>   What have you in your heart.
> Speak now, and I will answer;
>   How shall I help you, say;
> Ere to the wind's twelve quarters

I take my endless way.

The narrator contemplates generational time. The lives of individuals and the rural community in which they live are marked by the annual production of the harvest and by the births, marriages, and deaths of those who plant and reap those harvests and are in turn buried in country churchyards. It is the natural cycle of copulation, birth, and death, which means that humans begin in a state of non-being and return to that state at death. Just like every other living thing (flora or fauna), humans come from the earth and return to the earth – ashes to ashes, dust to dust. There is no suggestion of salvation and eternal life in these lines, just a sense of acceptance and calm resignation.

The description of the evolution of houses symbolizes the human lifespan. A rush of verbs in lines 1 and 2 suggests the pace at which all kinds of changes and modifications, both deliberate and accidental, are made. "Old stone to new building" (5) recalls the way local people took stones from Hadrian's Wall in the North of England and repurposed them for their own building projects – something that has happened throughout human history. Old building timbers are used to create "new fires" (5), but in the end, everything returns "to ashes, and ashes to the earth" (6). The earth is "already flesh, fur and faeces" (7), being composed of organic matter to which the organic matter of the dead returns be it "Bone of man and beast, cornstalk and leaf" (8).

This cycle is presented as an unalterable reality to which humans must submit. In these lines, humanity is a part of a cycle that involves every living thing on earth. The reference to "old timber" giving way to "new fires" recalls the fate of the manor house called Burnt Norton, which burned down. The section ends on a negative note by describing the wind blowing out the loosened glass panes and shaking the wainscot and "tattered arras (13). It seems that the wind will outlast humanity. This section is full of lists (verbs, nouns), and the last four lines begin with "And…" The effect of repetition is to suggest the generational pattern of life in which there is something reassuring. There is nothing spiritual in it. It is the pattern of linear time repeated from generation to generation, but still, it suggests that the individual human life is not entirely lived alone. There is a striving for pattern and permanence.

Part I, Lines 14– 23 ("In my beginning … the early owl.")

Notes

"refracted" (21) – Deflecting the straight path of a ray of light." The opposite of the experience in the rose garden, described in *Burnt Norton* where the sun reflecting off the empty pool created the momentary illusion that it was full.
"dahlias" (22) – A brightly colored garden flower with long, thin petals that form the shape of a ball.

Commentary

By returning to his ancestral village, the narrator exemplifies the cycle of life, which, he is fully aware, takes place in the context of the earth's continual metamorphosis as it orbits around the sun. East Coker is, in purely terrestrial terms, his beginning and will be his end. The description of dusk in the countryside provides a symbol for a person (presumably the narrator) somewhat past middle age. The coming darkness represents the death to come and perhaps also the dark night of the soul. The darkness comes first to a "deep lane" (15) in which the speaker is walking hemmed in by steep banks topped by hedgerows and overarching branches on each side. The lane sunken into the earth symbolizes life trapped in linear time in an image that echoes that of the world moving "on its metalled ways / Of time past and time future" (*Burnt Norton*, 125-126). Those who know East Coker will recognize this as an accurate description of the narrow sunken lanes that lead to the village.

The lane is narrow, and anyone in it has literally to press themselves against one of the banks to allow a van to pass safely. Like the image of railway lines used earlier, the lane symbolizes the speaker's constriction – there is nowhere else to go but where the lane leads, which happens to be to the village. The lane, then, represents the chronological path on which all humans are set. So, we are all trapped on a road that inevitably leads to our end – non-consciousness, which was also our beginning.

The heat (which was also a factor in *Burnt Norton*) appears to have hypnotized the speaker. The "grey stone" absorbs rather than redirects the sunlight (21), and the "dahlias sleep in the empty silence" (22). Unlike the description of the hectic city in *Burnt Norton*, this scene is tranquil, but unlike the garden, here it seems to offer no transcendent vision and no promise of resurrection. Everything appears to be in suspended animation, waiting for the first hoot of "the early owl" (23), a nocturnal hunting bird that may symbolize death.

Part I, Lines 24 – 51 ("In that open … In my beginning.")

Notes

"The association of man and woman […] Whiche betokeneth concorde" (28-33) – This passage is from *The Boke Named the Governour* (1530) by Sir Thomas Elyot (1490-1546), also an ancestor of T. S. Eliot from East Coker (though I have been unable to establish any link with East Coker). In this passage, Elyot defends dancing against the charge that it is necessarily reprehensible. This idyllic, timeless picture of people dancing around a bonfire to celebrate a marriage precedes the turbulent Reformation by just a few years. King Henry VIII's decision to reject the authority of the Pope and make himself head of the Church of England would disrupt the lives and faith of the English people for centuries.

Commentary

This section begins with a vision of country dancing in the open field on "a summer midnight" (25). It is a typically English scene, almost a rustic cliché, by no means original to Eliot. Compare the final poem in *Last Poems* by A. E. Housman, XLI Fancy's Knell:

> When lads were home from labour
>   At Abdon under Clee,
> A man would call his neighbor
>   And both would send for me.
> And where the light in lances
>   Across the mead was laid,
> There to the dances
>   I fetched my flute and played.
>
> Ours were idle pleasures,
>   Yet oh, content we were,
> The young to wind the measures,
>   The old to heed the air;
> And I to lift with playing
>   From tree and tower and steep
> The light delaying,
>   And flute the sun to sleep.
>
> The youth toward his fancy
>   Would turn his brow of tan,
> And Tom would pair with Nancy
>   And Dick step off with Fan;
> The girl would lift her glances
>   To his, and both be mute:
> Well went the dances
>   At evening to the flute.
>
> Wenlock Edge was umbered,
>   And bright was Abdon Burf,
> And warm between them slumbered
>   The smooth green miles of turf;
> Until from grass and clover
>   The upshot beam would fade,
> And England over
>   Advanced the lofty shade.
>
> The lofty shade advances,
>   I fetch my flute and play:
> Come, lads, and learn the dances
>   And praise the tune to-day.

> To-morrow, more's the pity,
>   Away we both must hie,
> To air the ditty,
>   And to earth I.

The narrator continues to draw the reader into the experiences he is describing. We were with him in the lane dodging those vans, and now we are looking over the fields just outside the village watching the rustics dancing – young men and young women, and husbands and wives. We are warned, however, that we must "not come too close" (24), for we are watching the spirits of the villagers of the past, and if they sense our presence, they will (presumably) vanish.

The pipes (ancient Greek pan pipes surely) are heard faintly, as is the beating of the "little drum" (26). The poet switches to archaic Elizabethan English. This indicates that what the narrator sees in his mind's eye is a marriage celebration that goes back centuries. Marriage is "A dignified and commodiois sacrament. / Two and two, necessarye coniunction" (30-31). It is the necessary prologue to procreation and an essential part of the life cycle on the planet. The dancers are people of the soil in two senses. First, their "heavy … clumsy shoes" (36) are caked with the "loam" (37) in which they work to grow their crops. Second, we are witnessing the mirth of people "long since under earth / Nourishing the corn" (38-39). This describes the cycle of organic material returning to the earth to fertilize new growth. As Mr. Keating says when he shows the students in his English class photographs of former school students now dead:

> [W]e're food for worms, lads! Because we're only going to experience a limited number of springs, summers, and falls. One day, hard as it is to believe, each and every one of us is going to stop breathing, turn cold, and die! […] Because, you see, gentleman, these boys are not fertilizing daffodils. (*Dead Poet's Society*, 1989)

The villagers dance "around the bonfire" and "Round and round the fire" (27, 33). The dancing represents the cycles of the seasons; the pattern of the dance has not changed for centuries. The dancers give their total commitment to the present moment, something the narrator thinks is virtually impossible in the modern era, as he has explained in *Burnt Norton*. Their dancing connects them to nature in a way that modern people have lost. However, they are "Keeping time, / Keeping the rhythm in their dancing" (39-40). The rustics are tuned into the patterns of nature, "The time of the seasons and the constellations / The time of milking and the time of harvest" (42-43). The dance is in tune with the cycle of the seasons dictated by the movement of the heavens. Here is no transcendent moment such as the speaker experienced in the garden of Burnt Norton.

Another day dawns, for it is not yet the narrator's time to die. Earth prepares for a new day of "heat and silence" (48), and the narrator similarly prepares because each new day is a new beginning. He is "here. / Or there, or elsewhere" (49-50), for life must be about movement in the wider pattern of existence. It really does not matter where he is. As the Goons Show has it, "'What are you doing here?' 'Everybody's got to be somewhere!'" ("The Goon Show" BBC Radio, 1950s)

Summary of Part I

The setting is one of the deep, narrow lanes leading to the village of East Coker. In an open field just outside the village, the narrator shows us the spirits of countryfolk who, hundreds of years ago, danced at a wedding celebration. All of these people were made of the dirt of the fields in which they labored, and they have long ago returned to the dirt from whence they came. Nevertheless, the speaker seeks them again in his mind's eye, a timeless dance to the music of the seasons in the midst of a dark world in which all things decay. Day succeeds day: night is followed by dawn. There is no hint that after death will come resurrection or of any meaning behind existence, but each new dawn *is* a new beginning.

Part II, Lines 51 – 67 ("What is the late … ice-cap reigns.")

Notes

"snowdrops" (54) – Snowdrops are perennial flowers with white blossoms. They can flower in early spring, autumn, and winter, depending on the variety.

"hollyhocks" (55) – Hollyhocks are cottage garden plants that bloom in a wide variety of colors on long stalks throughout the summer.

"triumphal cars" (59) – A chariot of war or triumph was called a car. This is a reference to the constellation *Auriga*, the Latin word for 'charioteer.' There is a Tarot card called "The Chariot" that Eliot might have had in mind since he was familiar with the Tarot pack.

"Scorpion" (61) – Scorpius is a star constellation and also one of the twelve signs of the zodiac.

"Comets weep" (63) – Comets are bodies composed of frozen gases, rock, and dust that orbit the Sun. Seen from the earth, they appear to have a tail consisting of gases.

"Leonids fly" (63) – The Leonids are spectacular meteor showers in the night sky that tend to recur every thirty-three years. Meteors and comets have traditionally been seen as harbingers of ill-fortune.

"vortex" (65) – A vortex is a circulating mass of air or water that sucks everything toward its center. "[The Stoics say that] at certain fated times the entire world is subject to conflagration, and then is reconstituted afresh. But the primary fire is as it were a seed which possesses the principles (*logoi*) of all things and the causes of past, present, and future events. The nexus and succession of these is Fate, Knowledge, Truth, and an inevitable and inescapable Law of what exists. In this way, everything in the world is excellently organized as in a perfectly

Study Guide

ordered society." (Eusebius, *Praeparatio evangelica* 15.14.2 quoting Aristocles)

Commentary

The narrator examines a paradox: it is late November, but the weather and the vegetation suggest spring, summer, and winter all at once. The low-growing snowdrops (in England called the 'fair maids of February' suggesting their flowering date) are blossoming and "writhing under feet" (54). The summer-blooming hollyhocks are reaching up to the grey sky and tumbling down as the weight of the blossoms becomes too great for the thin stalks to carry. The "Late roses [are] filled with early snow" (58). In the middle of life everything appears to be on a self-destructive path. All of this seems to be a symbolic way of the narrator reflecting on the paradox of his own life: he is beyond middle age yet still feels the same emotions and impulses that he did in his youth while also being aware of his approaching death.

The chaotic activity on the earth is mirrored by that in the heavens. The thunder that "rolled by the rolling stars" (58) suggests the sound of chariot wheels as the constellations fight against the sun and moon. "Scorpion fights against the Sun" (61), and ill-omened comets and meteor showers fly through the sky. The world and the universe are caught in "a vortex" (66) that will lead to "destructive fire / Which burns before the ice-cap reigns" (66-67). This suggests a disastrous period of global warming before the coming of another ice age. Ice ages have occurred in the past, and we have every reason to anticipate that they will occur in the distant future. A full ice age would basically end civilization in North America and Europe. However, when Eliot was writing, the Second World War seemed to have the potential to do that, not with ice but with fire. London would soon be burning down every night. Two atomic bombs would be dropped on Japan. (On August 6, 1945, the United States dropped an atomic bomb on Hiroshima, and three days later, a second was dropped on Nagasaki.)

I am reminded of the poem "Fire and Ice" by American poet Robert Frost:

> Some say the world will end in fire,
> Some say in ice.
> From what I've tasted of desire
> I hold with those who favor fire.
> But if it had to perish twice,
> I think I know enough of hate
> To say that for destruction ice
> Is also great
> And would suffice.

The essence of the world in time is that, although it turns in regenerative cycles, it will eventually disappear. This sounds very much like the apocalyptic vision of W. B. Yeats (1865-1939) in "The Second Coming" (1919):

> Turning and turning in the widening gyre

72

> The falcon cannot hear the falconer;
> Things fall apart; the centre cannot hold;
> Mere anarchy is loosed upon the world,
> The blood-dimmed tide is loosed, and everywhere
> The ceremony of innocence is drowned;
> The best lack all conviction, while the worst
> Are full of passionate intensity.

The cyclical pattern of nature is real, but it offers no permanence, no access to the transcendent. Each spring is not actually a return to the first spring but a chance to begin again. The cycles progress through time; they are not stationary. In this way, they offer a deceptive consolation because the natural cycle will ultimately prove to be self-destructive as it has in the past (e.g., the last ice age). The narrator does not say this here, but against this recurring pattern of destruction stands the still point that is the Word of God. God does not experience progression or cycles but dynamic stillness.

Part II, Lines 68 – 100 ("That was a way … humility is endless.")

Notes

"periphrastic study" (69) – Roundabout, longwinded, torturous.

"Bequeathing us" (77) – Leaving us after their death.

"hebetude " (78) – Dullness, stupidity, mental lethargy.

"In the middle, not only in the middle of the way / But all the way …" (89-90) – Compare Dante, *Divine Comedy*: Inferno, Canto I:

> In the midway of this our mortal life,
> I found me in a gloomy wood, astray
> Gone from the path direct: and e'en to tell,
> It were no easy task, how savage wild
> That forest, how robust and rough its growth,
> Which to remember only, my dismay
> Renews, in bitterness not far from death.
> Yet, to discourse of what there good befel,
> All else will I relate discover'd there.

"bramble" (90) – A bramble is any rough, tangled, thorny shrub, or in this case, an area of such shrubs.

"grimpen " (91) – As a common noun, 'grimpen' does not exist in the English language, though whether Eliot was aware of this, I do not know. Sir Arthur Conan Doyle (1858-1930) first used the world in his Sherlock Holmes novel *The Hound of the Baskervilles* (1901/2). Grimpen is a parish and hamlet on Dartmoor in Devon, England, and the Grimpen Mire, where the novel's villain Stapleton hid his hound, is nearby. As a verb 'to grimp' means to clamber or climb, this suggests that a 'grimpen' is where one might easily lose one's footing and fall.

"fancy lights" (92) – The will-o'-the-wisp occurs under various names in European folklore. It refers to the light of a lantern being used by supernatural creatures such as pixies or fairies to mislead travelers to their doom. Like the end of the rainbow, it seems to offer hope that does not materialize. The scientific explanation is that light is produced by rising gasses produced by the decay of organic material.

"Do not let me hear / Of the wisdom of old men, but rather of their folly, / Their fear of fear and frenzy" (93-95). Compare Thoreau, "Age is no better, hardly so well, qualified for an instructor as youth, for it has not profited so much as it has lost. One may almost doubt if the wisest man has learned anything of absolute value by living. Practically, the old have no very important advice to give the young, their own experience has been so partial, and their lives have been such miserable failures [...] I have yet to hear the first syllable of valuable or even earnest advice from my seniors" (*Walden*, 1.10).

"humility is endless" (100) – Compare Thoreau, "Humility like darkness reveals the heavenly lights" (*Walden* 18.13).

Commentary

The speaker reflects upon what he has just written and is dissatisfied with it. There is some self-deprecating humor in his assessment that he has written in a circumlocutory manner using a "worn-out poetical fashion" (69). There is also surely conscious ironic humor in the comment that the preceding lines leave the reader "still with the intolerable wrestle / With words and meanings" (69-70). In reality, those lines are among the easiest to understand in the poem so far! To the speaker, the "poetry does not matter" because what matters is the meaning that the poetry was attempting to communicate (71). If the words fail to get that meaning across to the reader, all the poetic technique counts for nothing. Nor is the narrator writing exclusively about his effort to write poetry. The struggle to use language to understand, make sense of, and communicate the human condition engages the poet and every other thinking, feeling human being.

Now, however, he does state his meaning very clearly, "It was not (to start again) what one had expected" (72). The narrator has not actually been talking about the confused mixture of the seasons or the disturbance in the heavens. That was an image to describe his own state. By it, he means that his late middle age is not proving to be the time of quiet "autumnal serenity" that he had been led to expect (74). It has not brought "the long looked forward to, / Long hoped for calm, the autumnal serenity / And the wisdom of age" (74-75). It seems that the elders deliberately deceived "us" (for the speaker is not only speaking of his own experience but also, presumably that of the reader), or perhaps they simply deceived themselves. If we believe them, despite the evidence to the contrary that experience provides every day, then we are a "receipt [recipe] for deceit" because we have bought into their lies (77). There is no "serenity" (78) except deliberate imbecility. The elders had not "wisdom" but the knowledge of "dead secrets" (79) that are of no use. Looking back into the past offers no wisdom by which to live one's life in the present and future.

Speaking from the perspective that his age gives him (Eliot was in his early fifties), the narrator calls into question the truism that the elderly are wise because they have experienced so much. The fallacy of this is that "knowledge imposes a pattern, and falsifies, / For the pattern is new in every moment" (84-85). As we look back on what we have experienced, we rationalize it by seeking to impose a pattern rather than accept the past as a series of random and unconnected incidents. We tend to assume that this is a sign of our deep knowledge, but the narrator identifies two problems. First, we do not so much remember the past as imaginatively recreate it in the present. In doing so, we "falsify" the past by imposing meanings upon it that it does not have. Second, the pattern we construct through our re-creation changes "every moment" because the world is continually changing (85). It lacks any consistency over time because it exists only in our present consciousness. As a result, moment by moment, "We are only undeceived / Of that which, deceiving, could no longer harm" (87-88). Our constant re-patterning of the past is of no real consequence because it has zero relevance to our present.

Thus, old men are trapped in their memories as in the middle of a dark wood, or a growth of brambles, or with their feet on the slippery edge of a marsh. We have "no secure foothold" (91) when we reimagine the past, trying to find meaning in our memories. In doing so, we risk encountering terrifying monsters or being enchanted by "fancy lights" (92) – a reference to the folklore tradition of the will-o'-the-wisp (*ignis fatuus*), a ghost light seen in the air by travelers at night, especially over bogs, swamps, or marshes. It is all meaningless. As B. Rajan explains, "The past is irrelevant as a means of judging the present. The sense of history, of kinship and community in time, can no longer interpret the urgencies which drive us" ("The Unity of the Quartets" in Rajan Ed. 83).

The speaker ends this section by denouncing the idea of the "wisdom of old men," which strikes him as a form of arrogance (94). In his experience, old men are foolish and fearful because they fear being possessed by "another, or […] others, or […] God" (95). Perhaps what they fear is becoming dependent on others as they get older and incapable of living independently. Ultimately, they fear death, which is a total loss of agency and places one in the hands of God. The harsh 'f' alliteration pounds home his point.

In contrast to the arrogance of the idea that old men are wise, the speaker insists that the only true wisdom is "the wisdom of humility: humility is endless" (93). The contrast here is between the short life of mortal man and the infinite:

> The houses are all gone under the sea.
> The dancers are all gone under the hill. (99-100)

True knowledge would appear to reside in the understanding that we know nothing. The pattern of the community as expressed in the country dance, the narrator's attempt at poetry, and the patterns that old men impose on past experience all fail.

Summary of Part II

The narrator begins by describing disorder among the seasons. In late autumn (i.e., November), it is as if spring has completely bypassed winter or summer has lingered. The speaker follows this with an apocalyptic image of the disordering of the universe at the end of the world. Man tries to discern some pattern in all of this flux, but poetry and language are inadequate to express it, and the wisdom that men claim to get from experience is false. The problem is the patterns that humans impose on life are based on what they have learned from life's experiences. However, because every moment is new, past experiences are inadequate to understand the present, so we falsify. Once we realize that even the wisest men have their share of folly and fear, we see that the only answer is "the wisdom of humility."

Part III, Lines 101 – 133 ("O dark dark ... death and birth.")

Notes

"the vacant into the vacant" (102) – The spiritually empty busy, important, worldly people will disappear into dark void of death that all will enter.

"Almanach de Gotha" (107) – First published in 1763 by C.W. Ettinger in Gotha, Thuringia, this lists the royal families, aristocracy, and prominent people of every European nation. It came to an end with the Soviet occupation of the former Saxon Duchies of Saxe-Coburg-Gotha in 1945. However, since 1998, it has been published in London.

"Stock Exchange Gazette" (108) – This was a periodical published in London from 1901 to 1967.

"Directory of Directors" (108) – This would be a Who's Who of the business world.

"I said to my soul, be still, and let the dark come upon you / Which shall be the darkness of God" (112-113) – This echoes a theme of the Psalms "Be still and know that I am God: I will be exalted among the heathen, I will be exalted in the earth" (*Psalms* 46:10, KJV), and "My soul, wait thou only upon God; for my expectation is from him" (*Psalms* 62:5. KJV). Also, compare St John of the Cross, *Ascent of Mt Carmel*, Bk 1, Ch 13, Nos. 10-13, in which he explores the exterior and interior kinds of spiritual purification:

> 10. As a conclusion to these counsels and rules it would be
> appropriate to repeat the verses in The Ascent of the Mount,
> which are instructions for climbing to the summit, *the high
> state of union*. Although in the drawing we admittedly refer to
> the spiritual and interior aspect, we also deal with the spirit of

imperfection existent in the sensory and exterior part of the
soul, as is evident by the two ways, one on each side of that
path that leads to perfection. Consequently these verses will
here bear reference to the sensory part. Afterward, in the
second division of this night, they may be interpreted in
relationship to the spiritual part.

11. The verses are:

To reach satisfaction in all
desire satisfaction in nothing.
To come to possess all
desire the possession of nothing.
To arrive at being all
desire to be nothing.
To come to the knowledge of all
desire the knowledge of nothing.

To come to enjoy what you have not
you must go by a way in which you enjoy not.
To come to the knowledge you have not
you must go by a way in which you know not.
To come to the possession you have not
you must go by a way in which you possess not.
To come to be what you are not
you must go by a way in which you are not.

12. When you delay in something
you cease to rush toward the all.
For to go from the all to the all
you must deny yourself of all in all.
And when you come to the possession of the all
you must possess it without wanting anything.
Because if you desire to have something in all
your treasure in God is not purely your all.

13. *In this nakedness the spirit finds its quietude and rest. For
in coveting nothing, nothing tires it by pulling it up and
nothing oppresses it by pushing it down, because it is in the
center of its humility.* When it covets something, by this very
fact it tires itself.

"wings" (115) – Wings are spaces off to the sides of the stage where actors wait
for their cues to enter. The wings may house a system for storing and changing
hanging scenery and store scenery needed during scene changes.
"an underground train, in the tube" (118) – The London Underground is
commonly called the Tube by Londoners. Most, though not all of it, is, as the

name implies underground, so that the sections between stations are pitch black. A train would have to come to a stop between stations to allow another train to exit before it can enter a station.

"under ether" (122) – Beginning in the early 19th century, ether was used as a recreational drug at "Ether Frolics" in the United States. Participants would cover their mouths and noses with ether-soaked towels, inhale through the cloth, and go into a euphoric state. Ether was first used as a surgical anesthetic in 1846 by William Thomas Green Morton (1819-1868), an American dentist and physician. With the release of safer and more reliable anesthetics in the 1960s, the use of ether declined. The side effects are similar to alcohol intoxication: dizziness, giddiness, euphoria, and central nervous system depression.

R. H. Ward describes an identical experience in the dentist chair. The anesthetic, in this case, was nitrous oxide (sometimes called laughing gas), but that does not change the significance of his description of what he experienced:

> I passed after the first few inhalations of the gas, directly into a state of consciousness already far more complete than the fullest degree of ordinary waking consciousness, and that I then passed progressively upwards (for there was an actual sensation of upward movement) into finer and finer degrees of this heightened awareness.
>
> But although one must write of it in terms of time, *time had no place in the experience.* In one sense it lasted far longer than the short period between inhaling the gas and 'coming round', *lasted indeed for an eternity, and in another sense it took no time at all* [...] I knew, I understood, I actually was, far more than I normally knew, understood and was. I put it in this way because I had no impression of suddenly receiving new knowledge, understanding and being. Rather I felt that I was rediscovering these things, which had once been mine, but which I had lost many years before. While it was altogether strange, this new condition was also familiar; it was even in some sense my rightful condition [...]
>
> Meanwhile, the extraordinary feeling of the *rightness of things* increased, became more poignant, and was accompanied as it did so by a peculiar sensation of upward and bodiless flight. This sense of upward movement continued until it seemed to me that I was rapidly passing through what I afterwords told myself was a 'region of ideas'. The emphasis had shifted, that is to say, from the emotional to the intellectual.
>
> One simply knew; and one knew not one thing here and another thing there, and all of them things quite unknown to ordinary consciousness; one knew everything there was to know. Thus

one knew also that everything was one thing, that *real knowledge* was simultaneous knowledge of the universe and all it contains, oneself included. It was perfectly true, what one had read in the books; in reality (as opposed to the comparative unreality in which we live) the All is the One [...]

According to our ordinary way of understanding we are used to relating to one another only things between which a relationship is sensually perceptible or logically calculable. Here relationships were of a different kind altogether. Things were related to one another which to ordinary thinking would have no connexion whatever, and related to one another in ways which we cannot normally conceive. Things which we should call far apart, whether in space or time or by their nature, here inter-penetrated; things which we should call wholly different from one another became one another [...]

Meanwhile, the 'bodiless upward lift' continued. The 'region of ideas' gave place to another of which I can only say that in it *everything came to rest in a perfection of light*. Here, while all was certainly living, *all was unchanging*. Here *at the heart of the sun stillness had it's being* [...]

By now I was sufficiently aware in the ordinary sense [...] I was once more able to think normally, to say to myself as the golden lines faded, 'So that's what it all means', and even as I said it to forget what it all means; I had 'regained consciousness' and with it an aching jaw and a vague impression of the dentist impatiently telling me to pull myself together. Yet a dim and apparently nonsensical echo of 'what it all means' did remain in my head. 'What it all means', I was urgently telling myself in the attempt to frustrate the swamping forgetfulness, is 'Within and within and within and...' repeated like a recurring decimal.

(R. H. Ward, *A Drug-Taker's Notes*, 1957)

"pointing to the agony / Of death and birth" (132-133) – This recalls the lines from Eliot's *The Journey of the Magi* in which one of the Wise Men describes his journey to Bethlehem to see the new-born Jesus and his subsequent return to his native kingdom. He reflects on the life-changing experience:

I had seen birth and death,
But had thought they were different; this Birth was
Hard and bitter agony for us, like Death, our death.

After this experience, the Magi could not go back to his old faith because that faith had died, and a new faith had been born – a difficult and painful process for

Study Guide

a mature man. The lines also recall perhaps *1st Corinthians*:

> But now is Christ risen from the dead, and become the firstfruits
> of them that slept.
> For since by man came death, by man came also the
> resurrection of the dead.
> For as in Adam all die, even so in Christ shall all be made alive.
> But every man in his own order: Christ the firstfruits; afterward
> they that are Christ's at his coming.
> Then cometh the end, when he shall have delivered up the
> kingdom to God, even the Father […] (15:20-24, KJV).

Commentary

The opening of this section reminds me of poem XXXII in *A Shropshire Lad*
by A. E. Housman:

> From far, from eve and morning
> And yon twelve-winded sky,
> The stuff of life to knit me
> Blew hither: here am I.
>
> Now – for a breath I tarry
> Nor yet disperse apart –
> Take my hand quick and tell me,
> What have you in your heart.
>
> Speak now, and I will answer;
> How shall I help you, say;
> Ere to the wind's twelve quarters
> I take my endless way.

Both Housman's and Eliot's narrator portray the life of man as a short
interlude between the "vacant interstellar spaces" from which his consciousness
was plucked and to which, deprived of that consciousness and therefore "vacant"
(102), he will return. The dark, in which man confronts the ultimate emptiness of
life, strips the soul of its pride and forces man to realize that it is vain to attempt
to discover any purpose or any meaning in existence. Only when man realizes
his true insignificance is he ready to begin to understand.

There follows a long list of the roles men (it *is* a very male-oriented list) play
in their lives. The emphasis is on the great in the spheres of business, politics,
art, and culture, but it also extends to include "petty contractors" (106). All die;
there are no exceptions, "They all go into the dark" (101). More shockingly, the
universe itself will eventually disappear into the darkness. The "Sun and Moon"
will simply cease to exist (105). Alongside this vision of a universal apocalypse,
there is some humor in the speaker's return to examples of the attempts of man
to bring pattern and order into his experience, "the Almanach de Gotha / And the

Stock Exchange Gazette, the Directory of Directors" (107-108). These examples of man's folly will likewise disappear. As Nasrulla Mambrol puts it, "The speaker's point is that in the hustle and bustle of the moment, when what is important to us comes near to seeming to have the same importance to the vast and impersonal universe, it is easy to be distracted and to forget the awful and persistent truth that no one and nothing survives very long" (Op. cit.). In death, the senses will no longer receive impressions, and man will no longer have the capacity to initiate action – all agency will be gone.

The message of universal mortality recalls John Donne:

> No man is an island,
> Entire of itself.
> Each is a piece of the continent,
> A part of the main.
> If a clod be washed away by the sea,
> Europe is the less.
> As well as if a promontory were.
> As well as if a manor of thine own
> Or of thine friend's were.
> Each man's death diminishes me,
> For I am involved in mankind.
> Therefore, send not to know
> For whom the bell tolls,
> It tolls for thee.

The funeral of one is the funeral of all. Yet ironically, every funeral is "Nobody's funeral" (111), an oxymoron, for the reason the Gravedigger gives when Hamlet asks whose grave he is digging:

> Hamlet: What man dost thou dig it for?
> First Clown: For no man, sir.
> Hamlet: What woman, then?
> First Clown: For none, neither.
> Hamlet: Who is to be buried in't?
> First Clown: *One that was a woman, sir; but, rest her soul, she's dead.*
> (Shakespeare, *Hamlet*, 5.1)

This helps to explain the paradox of the line, Nobody's funeral, for there is no one to bury" (111). We are not burying a person: the person no longer exists. When we go to a viewing of the body to say our goodbyes or to the funeral service to hear someone say what a great person he/she was, we are fooling ourselves. There is nothing to say goodbye to! Consciousness has disappeared into the vacant darkness.

All of this is a little depressing, not to say morbid, but at this point, the speaker introduces the idea of a transcendent being, a deity, God. Accepting the darkness as "the darkness of God" (113) allows him to acquiesce in his death, to still his soul, to allow the darkness to roll over him, and to trust in God to save him. Only by accepting our mortality can we achieve true humility and find a path to true spiritual fulfillment.

In an extended simile, the speaker compares the process by which the soul relinquishes the body to the scenery and backdrop being changed in a theater. The lights go out, there is the sound of rumbling in the wings, and we know that the backdrop of hills and trees and "the bold imposing facade" are being rolled aside (117). The next scene will have a different location. In the darkness, God is working; we cannot see God's working, but we can have faith in it. The narrator offers an alternative simile: when the underground train "stops too long between stations" (118), the darkness reminds us uncomfortably of the eternal darkness of death. We engage in meaningless chatter with the other passengers to cover our fear, but the people quickly run out of things to say. Every reader will know how uncomfortable it is when the conversation in a room suddenly grinds to a halt, and no one can think of anything to say. In the silence, on their faces, we can see the "mental emptiness" (120) behind each façade, "Leaving only the growing terror of nothing to think about" (121). The terror is not just of being tongue-tied. The people are face-to-face with the fear of *nothingness* after death because they have run out of things to distract themselves. It seems that humans are incapable of emptying their minds; they must fill their heads with trivia so that there is no room for a confrontation with ultimate nothingness. Humanity has not "come to terms with its own mortality, and is spending too much time fantasizing about immortality and self-importance" (Schmoop). That train again offers an image for the chronology of human life, just like the lane into East Coker. We live our lives on a treadmill that takes us from past to future with no time for the present.

The narrator offers a third simile. When people inhale ether, they are paradoxically "conscious but conscious of nothing" (122). This near-death state is as close as most of us will get to being dead, but it seems (at least to the speaker) to offer a solution. Emptying the mind (as in meditation) seems to be the narrator's aim. To transcend individual consciousness, one must escape the ego. The answer is just to wait for what is going to happen. This is hard since man is used to hoping and loving, but to do that now would be to hope for and love "the wrong thing" because the only things we are capable of conceiving of are things related to our earthly life, and they are irrelevant, even distracting (124 & 125). This is not the famous Kierkegaardian 'leap of faith,' which is a conscious decision to trust in the absurd; it is simply a waiting in faith. A Freudian psychologist would speak about giving up the ego, which Dr. Gregg Henriques describes as "your interpreter system, and it functions to develop explanations for your actions in the context of justification." We must abandon the concept of our *self* as being a person distinct from other persons and separate from the world because in death, that self will not exist.

Humans must wait, passive and empty, in faith; we must transcend thought because, paradoxically, he is "not ready for thought" (127). If we can achieve this state, then (more paradox here) "the darkness shall be the light, and the stillness the dancing" (128). In other words, having emptied our minds of meaningless junk, God will fill it with meaningfulness; having attained a still point in the turning world, we will experience the dynamic stillness of the dance. Thus, death will be the ultimate still point in the turning world; death will be where the dance is eternal. Every experience will be contained in that moment; nothing will have been lost of the "ecstasy" (131). Lines 129-131 list five life experiences that will exist in the same moment, "running streams [...] winter lightening [... the scent of] wild thyme unseen and the wild strawberry / The laughter in the garden." This moment will be "the agony / Of death and birth" in which our earthly self will cease to be, but we will be reborn eternally (132-133). The essential mystery of time and mortality will be open. The death of the body is the birth of the spirit.

Part III, Lines 133 – 146 ("You say I am ... you are not.")

Notes

"dispossession" (141) – This seems to be a reference to the story of the rich young man who asked Christ, "'Good Teacher, what good thing shall I do that I may have eternal life?" (*Matthew* 19:16, KJV) only to receive the reply, "Jesus said to him, 'If you want to be perfect, go, sell what you have and give to the poor, and you will have treasure in heaven; and come, follow Me.' But when the young man heard that saying, he went away sorrowful: for he had great possessions." (*Matthew* 19:21-22, KJV).

Commentary

This section is typical of Eliot at his most infuriatingly obscure. Here is also Eliot at his playful best, having his narrator directly address the reader, appearing to hesitate, appearing to ask for authorization, and then enjoying his own riddles. The diction is simplicity itself, and the sentence structures are clear and straightforward. There is not an image to be found and barely a poetic technique to be noted. The mystery is in the narrator's balanced use of antithesis, which draws on the verses of St. John of the Cross. The meaning, full of paradox, is elusive because language is inadequate to convey the experience.

To arrive at a moment of self-knowledge, a still moment yet within time, one must abandon "ecstasy" (137). That means we must give up the things of the world: memories, knowledge, plans, possessions – in a word, our *self*. As John Worthen explains, "'ecstasy' as humans know it is sexual; and, as such, inimical to a life of dedication and faith" (189). That, presumably, is why monks, nuns, and priests take a vow of celibacy. All of these things belong to the world in time, so it makes sense that one would have to relinquish them to step out of time. The starting point is to exist in the present moment. Of course, we have been in the present moment all along, so we arrive where we are, but where we are is where we are no longer are. We have been so tied up in rushing from past to future that we simply have not appreciated it.

More paradoxes! Since no human can actually conceive of what spiritual enlightenment will be, we must "go by [...] the way of ignorance" (139); that is, we need to dump everything we think we have learned in life (e.g., the wisdom of old men) because it is simply irrelevant. In order to attain the kingdom of heaven, we need to dump all of the stuff we have accumulated. At this point, we probably remember the image of the mud on the axel-tree of the wagon (*Burnt Norton* 48). Getting to this state of perfection will mean going "through the way you are not" (143); that is, we will have to embrace our ignorance and take a leap of faith (something we are not usually required to do when buying a newspaper or catching the 9 a.m. bus from the end of the street).

Summary of Part III

The speaker begins by acknowledging that we all go into that darkness of death. Yet that darkness is like the darkness in the theater between scenes in a play; we know it is a prelude to the next scene. That darkness is like being trapped on a train in the Underground; it will make us confront the vast interstellar spaces that we have spent our lives ignoring. That darkness is like being under ether; we are conscious without being conscious of our *self*. To achieve spiritual growth, we must go through the dark night of the soul. We must be still and wait without hope, without love, without thought, but only in humility and faith.

Part IV, Lines 147 – 171 ("The wounded surgeon … this good Friday.")

Notes

Part IV is written in an *ababb* rhyme scheme, one of the few examples of Eliot's use of traditional poetic structure.

"wounded surgeon" (147) – The Nicene Creed reads in part:

> We believe in one God, the Father, the almighty, maker of heaven and earth, of all that is, seen and unseen. We believe in one Lord, Jesus Christ, the only Son of God, eternally begotten of the Father, God from God, Light from Light, true God from true God, begotten, not made, of one being with the Father. Through him all things were made. For us men and for our salvation he came down from heaven; by the power of the Holy Spirit he became incarnate of the Virgin Mary, and was made man. *For our sake he was crucified under Pontius Pilate; he suffered death and was buried.* On the third day he rose again

in accordance with the scriptures; he ascended into heaven and
is seated at the right hand of the father. He will come again in
glory to judge the living and the dead, and his kingdom will
have no end

"distempered" (148) – Diseased.
"enigma" (151) – Every patient has a chart at the end of their bed on which are
recorded their vital signs (temperature, pulse, blood pressure, etc.). To most of
us, it would be a riddle or puzzle. However, it makes sense to the medical staff.
"The chill ascends from feet to knees" (162) – It was a traditional belief that the
dying body gets cold from the feet upward. This belief is reflected in Mistress
Quickly's tragic-comic description of the last moments of Sir John Falstaff:

> He parted ev'n just between twelve and one, ev'n at the turning
> o' th' tide; for after I saw
> him fumble with the sheets and play with flowers and smile
> upon his finger's end, I knew there was but one way, for his
> nose was as sharp as a pen and he talked of green fields. "How
> now, Sir John?" quoth I. "What, man, be o' good cheer!" So he
> cried out "God, God, God!" three or four times. Now I, to
> comfort him, bid him he should not think of God; I hoped there
> was no need to trouble himself with any such thoughts yet. So
> he bade me lay more clothes on his feet. *I put my hand into the
> bed and felt them, and they were as cold as any stone. Then I
> felt to his knees, and so upward and upward, and all was as
> cold as any stone.* (Shakespeare *Henry V* Act 2 Scene 3)

"purgatorial fires" (165) – Purgatory is an intermediate stage between life on
earth and eternal life in heaven. Catholics believe that it is necessary for those
who are going to be saved to pass through the cleansing fire of purgatory to attain
the degree of purity necessary for their souls to enter heaven. The Protestant
Church of England does not recognize the concept of Purgatory.
"roses ... briars" (166) – Some critics see these as representing respectively
divine mercy and divine judgment.
"dripping blood" (167) – The image is suggested by blood transfusion. The blood
drips from a bag.
"dripping blood" (167) and "bloody flesh" (168) – *Matthew* describes the
moment after Judas is identified by Christ as the one who will betray him:

> And as they were eating, Jesus took bread, and blessed it, and
> brake it, and gave it to the disciples, and said, Take, eat; this is
> my body.
> And he took the cup, and gave thanks, and gave it to them,
> saying, Drink ye all of it;
> *For this is my blood of the new testament, which is shed for*

many for the remission of sins.

But I say unto you, I will not drink henceforth of this fruit of the vine, until that day when I drink it new with you in my Father's kingdom.

(26:26-29, KJV)

This is the Eucharistic Prayer from the Holy Communion Service of the Church of England

Accept our praises, heavenly Father,
through thy Son our Saviour Jesus Christ,
and as we follow his example and obey his command,
grant that by the power of thy Holy Spirit
these gifts of bread and wine
may be unto us his body and his blood;

who, in the same night that he was betrayed, *took bread;*
and when he had given thanks to thee,
he broke it and gave it to his disciples, saying:
Take, *eat; this is my body which is given for you;*
do this in remembrance of me.

Likewise after supper he took the cup;
and when he had given thanks to thee, he gave it to them, saying:
Drink ye all of this;
for this is my blood of the new covenant,
which is shed for you and for many for the forgiveness of sins.
Do this, as oft as ye shall drink it,
in remembrance of me.

Wherefore, O Lord and heavenly Father,
we remember his offering of himself
made once for all upon the cross;
we proclaim his mighty resurrection and glorious ascension;
we look for the coming of his kingdom
and with this bread and this cup
we make the memorial of Christ thy Son our Lord.

"this Friday good" (171) – Good Friday is the day on which Christ's crucifixion of Jesus at Calvary is commemorated. On Easter Sunday, He rose from the dead:

For God hath not appointed us to wrath, but to obtain salvation by our Lord Jesus Christ,
Who died for us, that, whether we wake or sleep, we should live together with him.

(*1 Thessalonians* 5:1-2, KJV)

Commentary

More paradox – we can only be healed spiritually by the "wounded surgeon" (147). The narrator describes an operating theater, the surgeon using his scalpel to cut delicately and precisely into flesh. The scalpel "questions the distempered part" (148), trying to locate the site of the disease and cut it out. The wounded surgeon's ability to heal comes from his own experience of pain. The phrase "sharp compassion" (150) is an oxymoron: it transfers the adjective "sharp" from the scalpel to the surgeon's "compassion," conveying his strong motivation to cure and perhaps also his expertise in surgery. He alone is able to resolve "the enigma of the fever chart" at the end of the patient's bed into a diagnosis. (If you have ever seen the television series *House,* you will get the picture.)

The symbolism of the description identifies the surgeon as Christ who was crucified and died that men might have eternal life. *Isaiah* states:

> Surely He has borne our griefs and carried our sorrows; yet we esteemed Him stricken, smitten by God, and afflicte. But *He was wounded for our transgressions*, He was bruised for our iniquities; the chastisement for our peace was upon Him, and by His stripes we are healed. (53:4-5, KJV)

These verses identify Christ as the source of humankind's spiritual purification because he paid the price to heal us and restore us to fellowship with God. The "bleeding hands" result from the nails that pierced his palms as he was nailed to the cross, and another wound was that made by the spear thrust into his side by the Roman soldier as he hung on the cross at Calvary. In addition, Christ had bloody wounds to his head (from the crown of thorns), his back (from being whipped), to his ankles (from the nails that pinned his legs to the cross).

Yet more paradox! The only way to "health is [through] the disease" (152). This is not so obscure given the symbolism of the previous verse. If salvation is the only route to spiritual purity, then accepting one's sinful nature and one's inevitable death is the only way to achieve it by purging away the Original Sin inherited from Adam. This the "dying nurse" knows (153). This phrase has multiple meanings. The knowledge that one's nurse is dying is not usually comforting, but here it is. She is mortal like everyone else, but she is aware of it: she knows that "to be restored, our sickness must grow worse" (156). She is also the nurse *to* the dying: it is she who gives the dying the support they need as they 'transition.' Perhaps the nurse also symbolizes the Church (in Eliot's case, the Church of England). As an institution, the Church was in decline in the mid-twentieth century. In the modern world, faith in God is rather out of fashion (to say the least). I am reminded of the third stanza of "Dover Beach" (1851) by Matthew Arnold (1822-1888):

> The Sea of Faith

Was once, too, at the full, and round earth's shore
Lay like the folds of a bright girdle furled.
But now I only hear
Its melancholy, long, withdrawing roar,
Retreating, to the breath
Of the night-wind, down the vast edges drear
And naked shingles of the world.

Also, the Church has always been composed of mortal humans with the same imperfections as its congregants.

The form that the nurse's "constant care" (154) takes is not to please us but to remind us constantly that we are all sinners, the inheritors of "Adam's curse" (155). Only if we keep that in mind will we understand that salvation lies not within our power but within Christ's power, whom we must approach with humility. To be restored to health, "our sickness must grow worse"; that is, we must face the reality of how much we have fallen from the primal innocent state of Adam and Eve. We must face our sinfulness, not continue to keep evading it.

The next verse expands the image of the hospital to include the "whole world" (157) and the whole of humanity. Rich businessmen (again, in Eliot's day, it was almost exclusively men) often endow hospitals, an act of philanthropy aimed at raising their profile in society or gaining God's favor through good works. These same millionaires sometimes go bankrupt, victims of a downturn in business on the stock market. Here the "ruined millionaire" (158) would seem to be Adam who, by his sin, caused humanity to be exiled from the Garden of Eden and forced to live in a fallen world. However, the reference to "absolute paternal care" (160) brings us back to God the Father. The most relevant Scripture would seem to be *John* 3:16-21:

> For God so loved the world, that he gave his only begotten Son, that whosoever believeth in him should not perish, but have everlasting life. *For God sent not his Son into the world to condemn the world; but that the world through him might be saved.* He that believeth on him is not condemned: but he that believeth not is condemned already, because he hath not believed in the name of the only begotten Son of God. And this is the condemnation, that light is come into the world, and men loved darkness rather than light, because their deeds were evil. For every one that doeth evil hateth the light, neither cometh to the light, lest his deeds should be reproved. *But he that doeth truth cometh to the light, that his deeds may be made manifest, that they are wrought in God.* (KJV)

The idea that God "prevents us everywhere" (161) seems obscure. However, Merriam-Webster notes four archaic meanings of 'precents' that may be helpful: "a: to be in readiness for (something, such as an occasion); b: to meet or satisfy in advance; c: to act ahead of; d: to go or arrive before." The narrator seems to be saying that God holds us in his agape love, going before to prepare a place for us. As Christ said, "In my Father's house are many mansions" (*John* 14:2, KJV). Christ's sacrifice transcends time and covers the condition of humanity for all time (past, present, and future). Thus, it offers a transcendent permanence and meaning not to be found in the individual life or humanity's existence within the cycles of the universe.

In the third stanza, physical death is described as the body losing heat, and the fever affects the brain. This loss of heat is, however, a necessary prologue to being warmed in heaven. To achieve this, however, the soul must pass through the "frigid purgatorial fires" (165) – yet another oxymoron. These fires offer no warmth, for their purpose is to cleanse the soul of its earthly sin. This explains why "the flame is roses, and the smoke is briars" (166). The roses and briars have occurred in the poem before. They represent respectively the extremes of pleasure and pain encountered in life. Roses traditionally symbolize love, and briars seem to symbolize punishment. The body's weaknesses must be seared away if the soul is to have the purity to ascend to heaven.

The final stanza returns to life where "The dripping blood [is] our only drink, / The bloody flesh our only food" (167-168). The idea that humanity is flesh and blood reminds us that we are mortal and our time on earth is short. It also reminds us of man's inevitable corruption. Most of the time, however, man believes himself to be "sound, substantial flesh and blood" (144). This is a self-deception that we must overcome in order to be worthy of grace. Except when we are sick, we do not think much about death; we just go on with our lives as though they will go on forever. Despite this weakness, we still "call this Friday good," as though something inside of us recognizes the truth that we spend most of our lives ignoring.

The lines also carry a contrary message. They refer to the rite of Holy Communion (the Eucharist). Catholics believe that, through the miracle of transubstantiation, the Eucharistic bread and wine actually become the body and blood of Christ; Protestants see the taking of bread and wine as a symbolic act. (Religious wars were, of course, fought over this difference and millions of people killed.) By participating in this ritual, the faithful share in Christ's suffering and death, and therefore in his resurrection. That is why the body and blood of Christ is man's "only drink" (167) and "only food" (168). Only through them will we achieve spiritual perfection. For this reason, the narrator adds, "we call this Friday good" (145) because we recognize that Christ died that we might live. Nasrulla Mambrol puts it this way, "The notion that the day that the Christ was crucified is called Good Friday because of the benefit that Christians believe Christ's sacrifice brought to all humanity caps the entire movement toward the paradoxical with Christianity's ultimate paradoxical resolution" (Op. cit.).

Summary of Part IV

The narrator celebrates Christ's atoning death as embodied in the Eucharist. The paradox is that Christ died to give us eternal life, that he took on our sins to clean us of corruption, and that (for all its imperfections) His Church brings us spiritual health. To experience new life in Christ, we must first die. If we are to be warmed in the light of Christ, we must freeze in death and then be purified in frigid purgatorial fires. The way of eternal life comes through death – the death of Christ and our death provided that we put our faith in him. This is why we commemorate the day of Christ's crucifixion on Good Friday.

Part V, Lines 172 – 189 ("So here I am ... not our business.")

Notes

"l'entre deux guerres" (172) – Between two wars. World War One ended in November 1918, and World War Two began in September 1939.
"Trying to use words" (174) – Again, Colin Wilson is helpful:

> [Level 7 consciousness] is more than a peak experience: it is an odd sense of *mastery over time*, as if every moment of your life could be recalled as clearly as the last ten minutes. We suddenly realize that time is a manifestation of the heaviness of the body and the feebleness of the spirit. We can also see that if we could learn to achieve this condition of control permanently, time would become, in a basic sense non-existent. (*Beyond the Occult*, 482)

Wilson continues, "It is, of course, very pleasant to have mystical glimpses of the meaning of life, but what gives human beings really deep satisfaction is to *pin them down* in words so that they cannot escape" (Ibid, 490-491),

Commentary

This is one of the most lucid passages in the poem and one to which all readers of a certain age can relate (only the young might not be able to empathize with the narrator). It is really more prose than poetry but exquisitely formed prose. The opening line refers to the first line of Dante's *Inferno*, "Midway in our life's journey, I went astray." The middle-aged writer reflects upon the two decades between 1918 and 1939, the between-war years. During this time, he has struggled and failed "to use words" effectively (174). The essential problem is being caught in the onward movement of time, which means that the writer's skills are always outdated and obsolete. The writer develops both in the things he wants to say and the way in which he wants to say them, so "so each venture / Is a new beginning" (178-179). The skills he has developed over years of composition are of no use to each new challenge. This explains why he feels he has "largely wasted" (173) the last twenty years.

I find it interesting that lines 179 to 182 each contain at least one military word – perhaps the environment of war had seeped into Eliot's unconscious. The narrator speaks of his attempts to write as "a *raid* on the inarticulate" (179) undertaken, "With shabby *equipment* always deteriorating" (180). Here he laments that far from improving, his skills as a writer are in decline, just as a soldier's equipment, in immaculate condition when issued, must deteriorate while he is on active duty. Against "the *general* mess of imprecision of feeling" (181), he feels he can only throw "Undisciplined *squads* of emotion" (182). Ironically, there is no commanding officer in the modern world where feelings and emotions are like undisciplined soldiers running around leaderless. Feelings and emotions are always disobeying the writer's attempt to impose organization and pattern onto them with words. Writing is an unequal battle that the writer must lose.

Finally, the narrator uses the word "*conquer*" to describe achievement, victory, in writing (182) – that moment when, despite his conviction of inadequacy, the writer crafts something great. He aims to achieve this in the full knowledge that others have succeeded in the past, the greats of literature whom he "cannot hope / To emulate" (184-185), but he adds, "there is no competition" (185). All of the great writers are engaged in the same mission: to "recover what has been lost" (186). I think he means what we should call 'high art,' represented in literature by the greats like Dante and Shakespeare – writers we can never hope to emulate. Such artists produce works of art (a ceramic jar, a sonata, or a poem) that exist within time yet step out of time because they speak to the viewer/reader always in the *now*. Of course, sometimes these works of art are lost, and writers have to try to relocate the truths they embodied.

This is what the narrator is striving for, even in a time of war when "conditions [… / …] seem unpropitious," though he quickly pushes aside that excuse saying that the modern world represents "neither gain nor loss" for writers (187-188). This is because, for the writer, there is only "the trying" (189). It is not for the writer to judge his success or failure. (Those whose role it *is* to judge certainly were impressed. On November 4, 1948, T.S. Eliot won the Nobel Prize in Literature.)

Part V, Lines 190-209 ("Home is where … is my beginning.")

Notes

"old stones that cannot be deciphered" (196) – An obvious example would be the Rosetta stone discovered in the Nile Delta in July 1799. There are innumerable others.

"Old men ought to be explorers" (202) – Compare, "I would have each one be very careful to find out and pursue his own way" (*Walden* 1:100).

"petrel" (209) – Petrels belong to a group that includes a number of different types of seabirds.

"porpoise" (209) – Porpoises are marine mammals similar in appearance to dolphins.

"In my end is my beginning" (209) was the motto of Mary Queen of Scots (1542-1587), *"En ma fin est mon commencement."* Mary devised the motto after her imprisonment in 1568. She was executed for treason the following year.

Commentary

"Home is where one starts from," the narrator tells us, and home is where he is since East Coker is the place where his ancestors originated. As we grow older, we go out into the world and become increasingly aware of the complicated pattern within which our short lifetime is but a detail. The *now* is all tied up with past and present, and not just our own past but the history of people long gone, written in "old stones that cannot be deciphered" (196). The speaker tells us, "Not the intense moment / Isolated, with no before and after" (192-193). This obviously relates to the experience in the garden at Burnt Norton. That was an intense moment isolated, but it did not allow the speaker to entirely step out of time because it involved recovered personal memories. It failed to include the lives of others. Also, it was merely a fleeting perception. What the narrator seeks is "a lifetime burning at every moment / And not the lifetime of one man only" (194-195). Perhaps, however, that is the best that man can achieve – to experience an entire lifetime, an entire personal history, in a moment, so that time past and time future are always present. It is a glimpse of the spiritual state that is only possible through the grace of God.

The poem closes with a sense that the writer is reconciled to the human condition. Just as there is a time for birth, matrimony, and death in the vast cycles of history, so in an individual life there is a time for standing outside gazing at the stars and for staying at home looking at the photograph album. True love is not concerned with the "here and now" (201). John Worthen explains:

> For most people in love, the 'here and now' of each other are
> the very essence of feeling. But Eliot's new poetry insists that
> such love is to be given up in favour of a non-human love which
> has nothing to do either with the sexual or the everyday. (190).

Old men, however, should be explorers of "another intensity [/ ...] a further union, a deeper communion" (205-206). This seems to describe death, the inevitable next stage of being which is compared to a vast and stormy ocean. Since death is approaching, old men "must be still and still moving / Into another intensity" (204-205). What is left to the old to explore is not the world but the next stage of being.

Yet death is a return to the home from which man came for, "In my end is my beginning" (209). We "long for a final home in eternity where all things and all times are reconciled" (Scott Beauchamp). So it seems that the narrator is making a distinction between living our lives and preparing for the next stage of our existence.

Summary of Part V

The narrator reflects that he is halfway through his life and has basically wasted his time. His words and poetry both fail because language is inadequate to express what one wants to say *now*. Nasrulla Mambrol comments, "what is actually being challenged in such commentaries is the value that experience has for an ego-constructed self. Put simply, experience from a limited point of view, which is what the experience of any one human being is, is of very limited value" (op. cit.). Despite this, the "wisdom in humility" calls us to keep trying to find patterns and meaning in the moments of our lives. We need to still our minds from the distractions of the world and accept the stillness of death. We must be still moving, always seeking a deeper communion with God, for through the darkness of death, the resurrection will bring divine love and new life.

THE DRY SALVAGES (1941)

Preparing to Read

More mind-stretching!

1. Have you ever lived close enough to a river to have felt its impact on your life – whether beneficial or otherwise?

2. Have you ever lived close enough to the sea to have felt its impact on your life – whether beneficial or otherwise?

3. Do rivers and the sea have similar associations for you or very different associations?

4. Have you ever felt yourself to be in danger in water (sea or river)? What was it like?

5. What do you think happens after you die? Is that a question that you ask yourself a lot? Does it keep you up at night?

Part I Lines 1-14: ("I do not know ... in the winter gaslight.")

Notes

"the river" (1) – The Eliot family originated in New Bedford, Massachusetts, but Eliot's paternal grandfather, the unitarian minister William Greenleaf Eliot (1811-1887), moved to St. Louis, Missouri, in 1834. He became a civic leader, founding the Church of the Messiah and several educational institutions, including Washington University. Eliot's father, Henry Ware Eliot (1843–1919), became a successful businessman in the city, and his mother, Charlotte Champe Stearns (1843–1929), was a social worker who wrote poetry. T. S. Eliot was born at 2635 Locust Street, the last of six surviving children. In 1930, he wrote to the *St. Louis Post Dispatch*:

> It is self-evident that St. Louis affected me more deeply than any other environment has ever done. I consider myself fortunate to have been born here, rather than in Boston, or New York, or London. Of course my people were Northerners and New Englanders, and of course I have spent many years out of America altogether; but Missouri and the Mississippi have made a deeper impression on me than any other part of the world. I feel that there is something in having passed one's childhood beside the big river, which is incommunicable to those people who have not.

"strong brown" (2) – The Missouri River, popularly called 'The Big Muddy' because of its sediment, joins the Mississippi just above St. Louis, hence its brown color.

"implacable" (7) – Immoveable, intransigent, perverse, beyond control.

"rank ailanthus" (12) – *Ailanthus altissima* has many different names, including tree-of-heaven, stink tree, and Chinese sumac. It is an invasive plant: a rapidly growing deciduous tree native to China. The tree "was first introduced into the United States from England to Philadelphia, PA, in 1784. Extensive plantings in cities during the 1800's has resulted in its naturalization across the United States. An eastern range extends from Massachusetts, west to southern Ontario, Canada, southwest to Iowa, south to Texas, and east to northern Florida. It is found in less abundance from New Mexico west to California and north to Washington" (usda.gov).

Commentary

The poem discusses the nature of time and humanity's place in time by focusing on the element of water. The narrator says, self-deprecatingly, "I do not know much about gods," and then adds, "I think that the river / Is a strong brown god –" (1-2). This reminds us that the narration of *Four Quartets* is highly personal and speculative. (Later, the speaker will say tentatively, "I sometimes wonder if that is what Krishna meant.") This foregrounding of subjectivity, doubt, and speculation was important to understanding the poem.

Water has often been linked with the divine. The ancient Celts used to throw offerings into rivers, bogs, and lakes to appease the god(s) of the waters. In the following description, the narrator continues to personify the river, which is seen as inherently contradictory: "sullen, untamed and intractable," but also "Patient to some degree" (2-3); "Useful," but "untrustworthy" (4). Early in history, humankind had to work *with* nature, using the rivers as highways for commerce. As technology has developed, however, rivers have simply become an obstacle. Now engineers are challenged to build rail and road bridges across them. City dwellers virtually forget rivers. Nevertheless, the river keeps "its seasons," a reminder that our short time on the planet fits into the cycle of the seasons, which form a pattern of which we are a part.

This description might fit any major river on any continent but is particularly appropriate for the Mississippi, which, beyond St. Louis, enters its floodplain across which it meanders, constantly changing and posing problems for navigation bound for the port of New Orleans and the Gulf of Mexico. The Mississippi functioned for decades as the 'final barrier' between the white settlers and Indian Territory. As railways and roads developed, the Mississippi's importance as "a conveyor of commerce" (4) waned (though it never disappeared), and its significance as "a problem confronting the builder of bridges" (5) increased.

And so, at last, in the twentieth century, the river was largely "forgotten / By the dwellers in cities" (6-7). However, this was an error because the "worshippers of the machine" (10) had forgotten the primal forces of nature. The river god,

"Unhonoured, unpropitiated" (9), simply waited, plotting revenge. Eliot might have in mind any of a whole succession of devastating Mississippi floods in the nineteenth and twentieth centuries. The Great Mississippi River Flood of January-May 1927 inundated 27,000 square miles to depths of up to 30 feet and killed approximately five hundred people. The Great Ohio and Mississippi River Valley Flood of February-March 1937 inundated cities from Cincinnati to New Orleans and covered over 200,000 square miles to a depth of over 11 inches. It left around 350 dead and nearly one million homeless

The "dwellers in cities [...] choose to forget" the river (7-9). It is implied but not stated that the rural dwellers, particularly those who farm in the river's floodplain, are not so forgetful. Nevertheless, the river keeps "his seasons and rages" (7), and though seemingly unacknowledged, this "rhythm" is ever-present in the lives of those who live beside it. The river is present in everything they encounter throughout the year: the ailanthus in April, the smell of grapes in autumn, and even the family circle sitting around the gas lamp in winter. Eliot here seems to be drawing on enduring impressions from his own childhood.

The flow of a river is linear: it has a beginning, middle, and end – like the life of a human. Three aphorisms are attributed Heraclitus of Ephesus (who provides the two opening epigrams of the *Four Quartets*): "It is impossible to step in the same river twice"; "Ever-newer waters flow on those who step into the same rivers"; and "We both step and do not step in the same rivers. We are and are not." These ideas are frequently joined into one coherent statement, "No man ever steps in the same river twice, for it is not the same river, and he is not the same man." Heraclitus's point is that everything in the natural world is in a constant state of flux. Thus, both the river and the man are constantly changing; nothing is permanent. Of course, unlike a human, the river continues to flow season after season, year after year. It will outlive the men who build boats and bridges. As the narrator reminded us in *Burnt Norton*, the houses we build will eventually fall, and the same is true of our infrastructure. However, the river will still be there, which explains why the speaker thinks it is "a strong brown god" (2).

Part I Lines 15-48: ("The river is within … Clangs / The bell.")

Notes

"the torn seine" (22) – A large fishing net with sinkers on one edge and floats on the other that hangs vertically in the water and to catch fish that attempt to swim through.

"briar rose" (25) – The small-flowered sweet-briar rose is native to Europe.

"rote" (30) – Mechanical, unthinking routine or repetition. Here it refers to the repeated crashing of waves on the granite shore.

"heaving groaner" (32) – A buoy that repeatedly emits a warning signal rather like a foghorn.

"The tolling bell" (35) – The warning bell on a buoy – something like a large wind chime.

"anxious worried women" (38) – This is a reference to the Moirai, the three sisters of fate in Greek mythology. Working with other deities, the Moirai set the length of a person's life by spinning, measuring, and cutting its thread. The influence of this idea can be seen in Shakespeare's depiction of the Three Witches in *Macbeth* (1606) and in Joseph Conrad's *Heart of Darkness* (1899) which describes Marlow's visit to the shipping company in Brussels where he encounters women knitting.

Commentary

The river is contrasted to the sea: the former is "within us" and the latter "all about us" (15). This makes the sea sound much more threatening, as though it is hemming us in, which perhaps explains that, while the river may be "a strong brown god" (2), the sea has "Many gods" (25). It is "the land's edge" (16), as though it is an entirely foreign element. The sea reaches into "the granite" (16) of the land, suggesting that, no matter how hard and unyielding the land is, the sea will eventually overwhelm it. Although deep, mysterious, and primal, the river is something that can eventually be utilized, crossed, and subjugated. In contrast, the sea represents the endlessly unknowable and unconquerable. Traditionally, rivers are associated with life, while the sea is often associated with death.

The sea's creatures are evidence of "earlier and other creation," creatures that pre-date man and yet are still living (18), indicating a timescale against which human history (to say nothing of an individual life) is insignificant. It "tosses up" man's "losses" (22): torn fishing nets, shattered lobster pots, broken oars, "gear of foreign dead men" (24). The verb "tosses" suggests complete indifference. All of this shows man's weakness in his battle with the sea; not least, humans are mortal, and the sea is not. It may not be infinite, but it appears to symbolize the infinite. Unlike the river, the sea is not linear. If anything, the sea is circular, its various currents moving around the globe. This is another way in which the sea more fully than the river symbolizes eternity.

Unlike the river, the "sea has many voices, / Many gods" (23-24). It invades the land leaving salt on the briar rose and mist amid the fir trees. The speaker then lists the many sounds of the sea: the howl, the yelp, the whine of the strained rigging of ships as the waves beak, the distant sound of waves breaking against a headland, the seagull, and the "wailing warning" of the buoy indicating submerged rocks (31). The short lines ("The tolling bell," "Ground swell, a time," 35 & 37) are the waves crashing on the shore, and the long lines ("Measure time [...]", "Older than time [...]," 36 & 38) are the slow retreat of the water before the next wave. The image of a ship at sea in the fog symbolizes the human experience: we are adrift in a sea of eternity, without any way to get our bearings, where the past is gone, and the future is not yet here. The wailing is for our mortality; the warning bell in the buoy is our funeral knell. The devouring power of the sea serves to remind us that we will not live long. The natural world will eventually come for us all.

The sea exists in a different dimension from humankind. It "measures time not our time, rung by the unhurried / … a time / Older than the time of chronometers" (36-38). Humans count time in hours, like the "anxious worried women" (39) awaiting the return of their seafaring menfolk. The women spend the hours of nighttime "Trying to unweave, unwind, unravel / And piece together the past and the future" (41-42). They are desperately trying to undo the fate that the Moirai have decided upon for their menfolk. One can imagine them worrying about their future if their husbands should be drowned and wondering if there is something they should have done differently in the past. It is a fruitless occupation because "the past is all deception" (43) and the "future futureless" (44). All human attempts to make sense of life, to find some form or pattern of meaning in it, will prove useless. The women cannot bring together time past and time future in time present because death may rob them at any moment of their looked-for future. If the morning brings news of death, then for them, "time stops," yet for the sea, "time is never ending" (45). This shows the radical difference between sea time and land time.

The movement of the sea, "Clangs / The bell" (47-48) of man's mortality. Only by facing our mortality, which "is and was from the beginning" (46), can we begin to experience living. The conviction that we are in control leads us to waste time thinking about a future that might not happen and regret a past that cannot be changed. All that we really have is the present, and we must live in the present.

The preceding analysis explains B. Rajan's comment, "I know no poem more terrifying than *The Dry Salvages*" ("The Unity of the Quartets" in Rajan Ed. 83). Rajan argues, "In *The Dry Salvages* the limits of exploration are reached [...] The time which is measured by the bell 'under the oppression of the silent fog' is a time stripped of human specifications, an alien, pulsing and ultimate reality living all through and permeating all action" (Ibid, 83-84).

Summary of Part I

Since ancient times, rivers have been associated with life and the sea with death. The tolling fog bell that warns sailors of the location of submerged rocks recalls the tolling church bell of *Burnt Norton* (Part 4). Both are audible symbols of death. Here, the image of a ship lost at sea in the fog becomes an image for so much of the experience of our lives. We drift through existence without having got our bearings. We have lost touch with the past and cannot see into the future. The rocks of which the bell warns us might either be a place of temporary safety from the chaos from the sea or a place of danger and death.

Part II Lines 49-84: "Where is there an end ... the one Annunciation."

Notes

"the calamitous annunciation" (54) – The Annunciation, when Mary is told that she will give birth to the Son of God, is described in *Luke* 1:26-38:

> And in the sixth month the angel Gabriel was sent from God unto a city of Galilee, named Nazareth, To a virgin espoused to a man whose name was Joseph, of the house of David; and the virgin's name was Mary. And the angel came in unto her, and said, Hail, thou that art highly favoured, the Lord is with thee: blessed art thou among women. And when she saw him, she was troubled at his saying, and cast in her mind what manner of salutation this should be. And the angel said unto her, Fear not, Mary: for thou hast found favour with God. And, behold, thou shalt conceive in thy womb, and bring forth a son, and shalt call his name JESUS. He shall be great, and shall be called the Son of the Highest: and the Lord God shall give unto him the throne of his father David: And he shall reign over the house of Jacob for ever; and of his kingdom there shall be no end. Then said Mary unto the angel, How shall this be, seeing I know not a man? And the angel answered and said unto her, The Holy Ghost shall come upon thee, and the power of the Highest shall overshadow thee: therefore also that holy thing which shall be born of thee shall be called the Son of God. And, behold, thy cousin Elisabeth, she hath also conceived a son in her old age: and this is the sixth month with her, who was called barren. For with God nothing shall be impossible. And Mary said, Behold the handmaid of the Lord; be it unto me according to thy word. And the angel departed from her. (KJV)

Commentary

This section is a variation on the sestina form where the same rhymes occur in all six stanzas. The six, six-line stanzas rhyme on a fixed pattern of six closing rhymes (abcdef: ailing, -owers, -tionless, -age, -able, and -nation). The narrator asks the unanswerable questions: What is the end of the suffering of human existence? When will the suffering end? Life seems to be an unending succession of "soundless wailing" for the dead (49), of summer flowers that will wither and die in autumn, of human wreckage cast upon the shore, and of ancient bones tossed up from the sea of eternity.

Little wonder that Nasrulla Mambrol calls the opening of Part II "some of the most witheringly bleak poetry that Eliot, who can seem to be intimately acquainted with the dark side of human experience, ever penned" (op. cit). This reflection leads the narrator to two oxymorons, "the unprayable / Prayer at the calamitous annunciation?" (53-54). The reference here is not to the annunciation of Mary (although the use of that word must raise associations in the reader's mind). Every announcement of a pregnancy must be calamitous because "In my beginning is my end."

In Christian belief, the Annunciation refers to the angel Gabriel's announcement to the Virgin Mary of the Incarnation, observed as a feast on March 25. This is, of course, the very best of news to sinful humankind, but it carries with it the predestined death of Christ – "In my beginning is my end." It could also be any announcement of any pregnancy, for the birth of a mortal child is likewise the beginning of an inevitable calamity. The prayer would be for life and health, but it is "unprayable" because, just as the death of Christ was foretold, so too is the mortality of all men ordained. As the Bible says, "Man that is born of a woman is of few days, and full of trouble" (*Job* 14:1, KJV). The sea becomes a symbol for the hardships of human life: we are all destined to be bones, sharing the fate of Phlebas the Phoenician, "Those are pearls that were his eyes" (*The Waste Land*, "Death by Water").

The speaker acknowledges that his question has no answer: there is no end to the suffering of existence; there is only "addition" (55), that is, years added onto years, sorrow piled on sorrow. Humans spend their "Years of living among the breakage / Of what was believed in as the most reliable" (57-58). It is worth remembering that this was written when the war was destroying the British Empire on which the sun never set. Lots of things in which people had put their faith were literally crumbling before their eyes. That is the paradox of the human condition: we put our faith in temporal things (including people) because they seem "the most reliable" (59), but again and again, they are taken from us. The obvious lesson is that these very things are "therefore the fittest for renunciation" – we need to stop putting our faith in the wrong things. Humanity has to start letting go of the people, things, and values we deeply prize. It is only by renouncing the things of this world (the accumulated 'stuff' of our past and future) that we might be able to build our spiritual lives and find something reliable in which to believe.

Finally, if we live long enough, a person comes to old age, a time of "failing / Pride or resentment at failing powers" (61-62). Physical decline is the "final addition" (61) – the last in a long line of sorrows. We know ourselves to be consciousness trapped in a decaying, dying body, "a drifting boat with a slow leakage" (64), and so we try to detach ourselves from the things we are soon going to lose – first and foremost our ego. We listen for the final "undeniable / Clamour of the bell…" (65-66), which warns us that we are just about to hit the rocks and sink. This is the fate that was announced when someone first revealed a pregnancy. Perhaps the narrator also has in mind the death of empires. All past empires have risen only to fall, and at the time of writing, the end of the British Empire, and perhaps the end of Britain as a free nation, did seem to be pretty close.

It is not just the men sailing out from the New England harbors; we are all "fishermen sailing / Into the wind's tail, where the fog cowers" (67-68). What is to be *our* end? We know not when our end will come but only that it *will* come. The ocean (death) is always with us; neither our past nor future can have any "destination" (72). There is only the sailing of our finite existence on the ocean of eternity. We cannot conceive of a time when this vast, void of ocean will not be "littered with wastage," the wreckage of our "failed and vain human projects" (Schmoop).

The only way to avoid the terrifying existential truth of a short life lived out in a timeless, indifferent universe (compare "human kind / Cannot stand very much reality" *Burnt Norton*, 42-43), is to concentrate on the minutia of living, "bailing, / Setting and hauling" (74) – doing the things necessary to keep the boat afloat and life going, even in a storm. We *have* to imagine the fishermen getting on with their lives onshore, "drawing their money, drying sails at dockage" (76). The alternative would be to confront the reality of existence, a life that brings no final reward or achievement. It would be too painful to think of them as "making a trip that will be unpayable" (77); that is, making a trip from which they will never return with any "haul" worth examining (78). The narrator seems to be saying that we sleepwalk our way through life, allowing ourselves to get caught up in the day-to-day struggle to keep afloat. It is a form of self-protection. Thus, trapped in a sinking boat (the *Titanic* does come to mind), we spend our entire lives bailing instead of preparing ourselves spiritually for a death that is coming.

The speaker asserts that there is no end to earthly suffering; there is no end to earthly dying. Death is paradoxically called "the movement of pain that is painless and motionless" for those who die (81). In a world that provides no answers, where death is the only god that appears to have power, there is, "Only the hardly, barely prayable / Prayer of the one Annunciation" (83-84). The use of the capital 'A' is vitally important. The only hope is in the Christian message because, while the death of Christ was foreordained, so too was his resurrection. Thus, while "the bone's prayer [is] to Death its God" (83), there is an alternative for humanity – the soul's prayer to the Christ who promised resurrection. So, to the two criminals crucified on either side of him, Christ said, "Verily I say unto thee, Today shalt thou be with me in paradise" (*Luke* 23:43, KJV).

Part II Lines 85-123: "It seems, as one becomes ... is what it always was."

Notes

"ineffable" (100) – Incapable of being expressed in words.
"bitter apple" (117) – This may refer to Mark Twain's classic *Huckleberry Finn*, a novel set on the Mississippi River. At one point, has Huck and Jim vowing never again to steal and eat bitter persimmons ("the bitter apple") and stick instead only to stealing and eating watermelons. Hannibal, Twain's birthplace, is about one

hundred miles upriver of St. Louis.

"halcyon" (120) – This word describes an idyllic time in the past that is remembered as better than today – a time characterized by happiness, great success, and prosperity. The word also refers to a fabled bird, identified with the kingfisher, supposed to have had the power to calm the wind and the waves while it nested on the sea during the winter solstice. (Merriam-Webster and The Free Dictionary).

Commentary

This section opens with an important qualification, "It seems" (85). The speaker is giving his impression, and of course, impressions can be wrong. As one becomes older, he says, the past seems no longer to be merely a "sequence" of events (86) or even a "development" (87). Seeing the past as an upward progression is dismissed as "a partial fallacy" (87) that derives from "superficial notions of evolution" (88). Suppose we believe that things have been developing into a superior state (as in Darwin's theory of species whereby lifeforms constantly adapt to changing conditions and those which adapt best survive while the rest become extinct). In that case, the past can be disowned as something inferior; it can be left behind. That would be a mistake, presumably because the past served to make us what we are now.

To provide some context, Eliot had been born at the height of the pseudo-science movement called Eugenics. Wikipedia defines this as "a set of beliefs and practices that aim to improve the genetic quality of a human population, historically by excluding people and groups judged to be inferior or promoting those judged to be superior." Eugenics had resulted in some terrible practices in relation to people who were considered inferior, particularly those with mental problems. As awful as some of these actions were in Britain and America, they pale before the Nazi policies founded on the belief that Aryans were the master race and all other races were genetically inferior. These ideas led by way of mass forced sterilization of 'defective' individuals straight to the extermination camps, the Holocaust, and the deaths of millions.

The pattern the narrator means is visible to us in moments of peak experience. These are not to be confused with times when we feel good about ourselves or our lives. These are entirely trivial feelings, "the sense of well-being, / Fruition, fulfillment, security or affection, / Or even a very good dinner" (90-92). What he is talking about are moments of "sudden illumination" (92). We recall an experience, the meaning of which we "missed" at the time (93), and *now* suddenly, it seems clear to us. As they say in Britain, 'the penny drops.' We have an 'aha moment.' In such moments of insight, we relive the past in "a different form," which transcends simple happiness (95). Happiness is simply an evasion of suffering and mortality – a temporary refuge from the inevitable. What the speaker is trying to describe is a moment of insight into the nature of existence. This seems to be what the speaker experienced in the garden at Burnt Norton.

The key difference between mere memory and "the past revived in the meaning" (97) is that the past remembered in a moment of peak experience contains the cumulative experience "of many generations" (99). This certainly brings to mind the country dancing in *East Coker*. We understand what happened to us to be part of, on the one hand, "the assurance / Of recorded history" (101), and on the other, "the primitive terror" of death and infinity. There is something reassuring in seeing once again the dancers on the green. It shows us that our life fits into a multi-generational pattern. Yet there is something terrifying in the vision when we recall that the dances are all (in the words of Mr. Keating) "fertilizing daffodils."

Now we understand that our experiences of agony and pain are as permanent as are our moments of happiness – or, at least, as permanent as anything can be that happens in the world of duration. We learn this in these moments of illumination. Incidentally, it is pretty irrelevant what caused the agony, whether it was hoping for or dreading the wrong things. Ironically, the speaker notes that it is easier to see the significance of such agony in the lives of people we are close to than it is in our own lives. We tend to obscure our past agonies with subsequent actions and change, but we are not aware of these in others, so "the torment of others remains an experience / Unqualified, unworn by subsequent attrition" (112-113). Looking at people whom we know well, we see much more clearly how pain has shaped them and how it stays with them no matter how much they appear to change or try to smile through the pain. We know that "the agony abides" inside them, as it does in us (114).

The narrator explores another paradox, "Time the destroyer is time the preserver" (115). Time, which destroys so much, also preserves the agonies of that destruction. Similarly, the Mississippi that carries the cargo of commerce also carries the bodies of "dead negroes, cows and chicken coops" (116) in the memory of the times it flooded. The "bitter apple" also carries with it the memory of the bite in the apple (117). This refers to Original Sin when the serpent tempted Eve and Adam to bite into the fruit of the Tree of Knowledge. Such agonies are like the ragged rock (the Dry Salvages) amid the restless waters, hidden by fog and the waves. On perfect days, the rocks stand out like "a monument" (120); in "navigable weather," they serve as a seamark that helps us navigate our lives (121). But in winter or storms, they are what they always were, a sign of our sinful mortality, a message that we may be wrecked on the rocks of eternity at any moment.

Summary of Part II

We all have transcendent moments of sudden illumination within time, like the moment in the rose garden. They are often triggered by intensely vivid memories, but they are not mere memories. They are glimpses of eternity, but most of us do not realize their meaning. Similarly, our moments of agony serve as reminders of our sin, which, like a fog bell, help us navigate our lives through sin and repentance. Nasrulla Mambrol adds, "one must have more than memories colored by what one has overheard and read and otherwise acquired, the memories of others; one must have something permanent and fixed that is one's own, both to lay one's course by and to measure one's progress" (op. cit.)

Part III Lines 124-145 – "I sometimes wonder ... is before us.'"

Notes

"what Krishna meant" (124) – "Krishna and Arjuna in *The Bhagavad Gita* are two of the most important figures in the text. Prince Arjuna leads the Pandavas' army. His chariot is driven by Sri Krishna, an incarnation of the god Vishnu, who has taken a mortal form in *The Bhagavad Gita*. Krishna has been Arjuna's friend and advisor throughout his life, but he can't fight this battle. Leading the army is Arjuna's dharma – his duty and destiny. Krishna is only there to support him" (Shortform). "What Krishna hopes to teach Arjuna in this quotation is the importance of acting without thinking about how one's actions will benefit oneself. Like Arjuna, we must all learn to act in a way that reflects our spiritual respect for death" (Schmoop).

"drumming liner" (142) – The drumming is the sound of the engines and the screw churning in the water.

Commentary

The Hindu god Krishna teaches that the future is, in a sense, already past. To describe this future, the speaker uses the metaphor of an old book that contains some "wistful regret" (127), only the book has not yet been opened. People used to press flowers ("a Royal Rose or a lavender spray," 126) between the pages of books to preserve them as a memento. What we think of as the future will someday be someone's past. Someone will look back on a memory ("a faded song," 126) with "whistful regret" (127) just as we do. If Krishna is right, then that has already happened because our conviction that time is linear is false. The implication is that there is no point in us looking to the future for redemption: the future is going to be just like the past, full of beauty and loss and regret.

Krishna's concept of time is the opposite of the Western concept of linear chronology. Hence, "the way up is the way down, the way forward is the way back" (129). Since all time is always present, then "time is no healer" and "the patient is no longer here" (131). This is a version of Heraclitus' epigram, "It is impossible to step in the same river twice." The person who needs to be healed no longer exists because we are constantly changing. The narrator uses an extended metaphor to explain this. When passengers depart on a train journey, they settle down to their occupations, "fruit, periodicals and business letters"

(133), leaving their past behind because "those saw them off have left the platform" (134). The railway carriage is a kind of present, isolated from past and future and thus from "grief" (135). That is why the passengers relax to the "sleepy rhythm" of the train on the tracks (136). The speaker urges the travelers to "Fare forward" (137). These people have effectively stepped out of time. They are no longer the same people they were when they got on the train; they are not yet the people who will get off. They are traveling for no motive other than to fare forward cut off from past and future.

The future, the speaker has already established, is already written, and it will be more of the same. The only thing that will change is the individual because the people on the train "are not the same people who left that station / Or who will arrive at any terminus" (139-140). There is only *now*. So, people on a train should not look back at the "narrowing rails" (141) that appear to come together in the distance, just as people on an ocean liner (the speaker returns to earlier nautical imagery) should not look back on the "furrow [the ship's wake] that widens behind [them]" (142-143). He urges us not to "think 'the past is finished' / Or 'the future is before us'" (144-145). There is only the present, and the present contains the past (the station from which the train departed) and the future (the station at which the train journey will end), but we do not live our lives for them but for the *now*.

At night, the wind in the rigging makes the same sound as the swirling air in a conch shell. The sound urges on those who think they are voyaging, reminding us again that we are constantly evolving. The time on the train or on the ship, "While time is withdrawn" (153), is an opportunity to reflect that we shall never be the same people again. For this reason, we must make the most of the present experience, for "the time of death is every moment" (159). There is no point in thinking of the past with nostalgia, regret, guilt, or looking to the future with hope, dream, or expectations. Past and future must be thought of in the context of *now*.

Part III Lines 146-168 – "I sometimes wonder ... fare forward, voyagers."

Notes

"the aerial" (146) – I assume this refers to the antenna, a metallic rod for radiating or receiving radio waves. For obvious reasons, this is located as high on the ship as possible.

"fructify" (160) – Make to bear fruit, to be productive.

Commentary

At night, climbing in the rigging or the ship's aerial, we can hear a voice. We do not perceive it through our physical ear ("The murmuring shell of time," 148) because, being of the body, the ear is tied to linear time. The voice sings to us, urging, "'Fare forward, you who think you are voyaging'" (149). Actually, we are not voyaging. While on this ship, "time is withdrawn" (153); each moment is a moment out of time. We have escaped the day-to-day bustle of duration. We are not the same person who left the harbor and not the same person who will disembark. [If you think that Eliot is recycling the image of the train going from station to terminus, you are right.] The message is that we are freed from our dependence on time past and time future on the ship, between the shore behind and the shore ahead. We are in the still point, our lives suspended, neither acting nor not acting. In this state of stasis, we perceive that every moment of consciousness is the same consciousness one will have at the moment of death. In other words, life is totally meaningful because every second we might die, and our spiritual fate depends upon "'whatever sphere of being / The mind of man may be intent / At the time of death'" (156-158). Thus, only if we free ourselves from the tyranny of concern for the past and present, only if we "do not think of the fruit of action" (161), can we become true voyagers.

There is no point in calculating the advantages of one action or another action. That is to put our faith in the future. Instead, all voyagers and seamen need to cultivate the mindset that comes from facing our mortality. All of us are like sailors on the sea of eternity: some of us will reach port, and some will suffer "the trial and judgment of the sea" (164). No matter what happens, "this" is our "real destination" (165). "This" seems to mean the state of consciousness in which we can be intimately connected to the moment of our death. By not thinking about ourselves anymore in terms of the day-to-day world, we "shall fructify in the lives of others," presumably because it will make us less ego-centric (160).

Krishna admonition, "Not fare well, / But fare forward, voyagers" (167-168), is an encouragement to continue with our own spiritual development, not our progress in the world of mortals. Doing that will keep us humble and make the impact that we have on others much better. Eliot may have in mind here something like the Mother Teresa effect – the egoless saint makes the lives of all who come into contact with her richer and more fruitful.

Summary of Part III

The "future" is simply a "past" that we have not yet experienced. We need, therefore, to free ourselves from the pressures of both past and present. To do this, we need to think of ourselves as passengers of a train or on a ship. We board the train/ship in one location, travel for a while, and then get off in another location. We know that the place we left (our past) is still there, and we know that the place where we are going (our future) already exists. Nevertheless, while on the train/ship, we are free of the demands of the world of appointments and plans and regrets.

A person on the point of dying is at the Still Point that gives meaning to his or her life and the lives of others. However, our death could come at any moment, and therefore we must develop static consciousness by casting off all of the things of this world and concentrating on eternity. That makes sense of what Krishna told Arjuna: knowing that every moment may be the moment of our death (particularly in the midst of battle), we know that even the moment of death is not an end but a beginning into which we should fare forward.

Part IV Lines 169-183 – "Lady, whose shrine ... Perpetual angelus."

Notes

"Lady, whose shrine stands on the promontory" (169) – Eliot identified this shrine as the Church of Notre Dame de la Garde built on the foundations of an ancient fort at the highest natural point in Marseille on the south side of the Old Port, overlooking the Mediterranean. There are many such shrines on the coasts of Europe and America where prayers can be said asking Mary to watch over those who go to sea. In Gloucester, Massachusetts, a Roman Catholic church, Our Lady of Good Voyage, stands on a hill overlooking the inner harbor. This is the church to which Eliot would have accompanied his Catholic nurse, a young Irish woman named Annie Dunne, for Sunday Mass during the family's summer vacations there. He would also have been familiar with stories of New England fishermen who had been lost at sea.

"*Figlia del tuo figlio*" (177) – "Daughter of your own son" (i.e. the Virgin Mary) from Dante's *Paradisio*. This paradox is explained because, as an earthly mother, Mary gave birth to Christ, and so was his mother. However, as God (the Trinity: Father, Son, and Holy Ghost), Christ created Mary, who would therefore be his daughter.

"angelus" (183) – The Angelus is both the bell that calls the faithful to devotion and the name of a particular devotion of the Western church that commemorates the Incarnation (the belief that Jesus Christ is both fully God and fully human). It is recited in the morning, at noon, and in the evening.

Commentary

Nasrulla Mambrol comments, "While it may not be readily apparent, the *Four Quartets* have been continually tending toward a Judeo-Christian resolution in keeping with the foundational religious values and the traditional belief system not just of the poet but, more important, of the culture that formed him" (op. cit.). Another way of saying this is that *Four Quartets* is becoming a work of Christian mysticism ever more clearly.

This section is a lyrical prayer to Mary to intercede for the lives and souls of those who go upon the sea. However, this is merely a metaphor since the narrator also asks Mary to protect those who go about "every lawful traffic / And those who conduct them" (172-173). The reference in the first line puts me in mind of the Shrine of Our Lady of the Shipwrecked, which nestles against a rock facing the deep blue Atlantic Ocean in Finisterre, on the west coast of Brittany in France.

In her poem "Finisterre," Sylvia Plath describes it thus:

> Our Lady of the Shipwrecked is striding toward the horizon,
> Her marble skirts blown back in two pink wings.
> A marble sailor kneels at her foot distractedly, and at his foot
> A peasant woman in black
> Is praying to the monument of the sailor praying.
> Our Lady of the Shipwrecked is three times life size,
> Her lips sweet with divinity.
> She does not hear what the sailor or the peasant is saying —
> She is in love with the beautiful formlessness of the sea.

The similarities between Plath and Eliot are remarkable. Prayers are requested for the men who go out to the sea to make their living and the women who wait anxiously for their return. Prayers are requested for those who have been swallowed up by the immensity of the ocean whose "dark throat which will not reject them" (181) and those who are lying dead on the sand. Prayers are requested for those who are beyond hearing the sound of "the sea bell's / Perpetual angelus" (182-182). This is at once the bell that would have warned them of hidden rocks and guided them safely to their home port and the bell that would have called them to have faith in God to bring their souls safely into an eternity of his love.

Nasrulla Mambrol draws attention to the context in which *The Dry Salvages* was written, "At the height of the sea conflict, in May 1941, German submarines were sinking 300,000 tons of allied shipping, or in the vicinity of 10 or more seagoing supply vessels, weekly. In plain terms, death and destruction at sea were likely more numerous at the time of Eliot's writing than at any other time in human history..." (op. cit.).

Summary of Part IV

The speaker asks Mary to pray for those who go upon the sea (a metaphor for all humanity), and for the women who fear to lose, or have already lost, sons or husbands, and for the souls of those who have died at sea. The prayer asserts that life has no end without faith, only the accumulation of suffering and sorrow.

Part V Lines 184-198 – "To communicate ... in the Edgware Road."

Notes

"To communicate with Mars" (184) – Mars was once thought to be inhabited – because if not, who built the canals that are visible on the planet's surface? In astrology, of course, the planets are thought to exert a profound influence on human destiny. An individual's future would be predicted by casting their horoscope.

"converse with spirits" (184) – Spiritualism, the belief that spirits are able to communicate with the living through the agency of a medium, was still prevalent in the first decades of the twentieth century. The loss of so many young men in the First World War left grieving loved ones with a desperate need to believe that their spirits survived.

"To report the behaviour of the sea monster" (185) – This refers to mythical sea monsters like the Kraken.

"Describe the horoscope, haruspicate or scry" (186) – The position of the stars at the time of one's birth is supposed to have a significant influence upon one's life. Haruspication is divination by the inspection of the entrails of animals, very popular in Roman times. Scrying uses a crystal ball to discover hidden knowledge or future events.

"Observe disease in signatures" (187) – Diagnosing diseases by analyzing handwriting is one of the more rational of the ideas in this list. It is still in use.

"evoke / Biography from the wrinkles of the palm / And tragedy from fingers" (187-189) – Palmists, hand readers, hand analysts, or chirologists practice fortune-telling through the study of lines on the palm of the hand. Often associated with gypsies (Romani), the practice is widespread in cultures throughout the world.

"release omens / By sortilege, or tea leaves" (189-190) – Each of these methods of divination involves interpreting what a person sees. Omens are events in the natural world that are seen as predictive (e.g., the flight of birds or a black cat crossing one's path). Sortilege involves telling fortunes by picking lots (like picking a fortune cookie). Reading the tea leaves of a person's empty cup is a very British form of fortune-telling.

"riddle the inevitable / With playing cards, fiddle with pentagrams / Or barbituric acids" (190-192) – The riddle suggests the Oracle at Delphi, which always presented its predictions in the form of a riddle. Playing cards have often been used to tell fortunes, particularly the mysterious Tarot pack which also appears in *The Waste Land*. The pentagram has magical associations. Barbituric acid can form a large variety of barbiturate drugs that depress the central nervous system. I presume they have been used to induce receptive states for divination.

"dissect / The recurrent image into pre-conscious terrors" (192-193) – This is a reference to psychoanalysis. The two leaders in this field were Sigmund Freud (1856-1939) and Carl Jung (1875-1961). Psychoanalysis sought to interpret images that kept cropping up in patients' minds as symbolic clues to their subconscious psychological issues. Freud's *The Interpretation of Dreams* (1899) was a classic text. Of course, psychologists consider themselves to be scientific in their approach to understanding mental illness, so Eliot's decision to place them on this list rather indicates that he disagreed. He lumps together a range of psychoanalytical approaches: making a connection with the subconscious, regressing to the experience of the womb, exploring the death experience through necromancy, and the interpretation of dreams.

"Edgware Road" (198) – Eliot lived near this major road that runs for ten perfectly straight miles through London.

Commentary

The narrator describes, somewhat facetiously, the ways humans have attempted to divine the future. This is a topic that occurs in *The Waste Land,* notably with the clairvoyant Madam Sosostris (who sadly has a bad cold that she did not foresee – which is the poem's best joke) and the blind prophet Tiresias. There is no need to explain each reference to understand that the sheer scale of the list points to the absurdity of such superstitious, occult endeavor. As the narrator concludes, these "are usual / Pastimes and drugs, and features of the press" – virtually every newspaper ran a daily Horoscope (194-195). Dissecting "The recurrent image into pre-conscious terrors" (193) sounds a little like the Rorschach inkblot test, one of the most common psychodiagnostic personality tests, allowing a psychologist to investigate the mind of a human being and determine the nature of a psychological disorder. Eliot appears to have regarded psychiatry as pseudoscience on a par with the other examples.

None of these methods of divination is to be taken seriously, but while ever "there is distress of nations and perplexity" (197), people will want to know the meaning, the endpoint, the answer. We remember that Eliot was writing in the dark days of World War II. Notice the comic bathos of the line, "Whether on the shores of Asia, or in the Edgware Road" (199). The idea of world-shaking events in distant Asia (in this case, the expansion of the Japanese empire and the attack on Pearl Harbor) is just about conceivable. The idea of such an event on the familiar Edgware Road is rather absurd, yet it was happening nightly during the Blitz.

Part V Lines 199-233 – "Men's curiosity stretches ... of significant soil."

Notes

"Men's curiosities [...] the moment in and out of time" (199-207) – Deborah Leiter argues that the following passage from *Walden* "is key in that its sense, its words, and its call to action are all echoed many times in *Four Quartets*":

> God himself culminates *in the present moment*, and will never be more divine *in the lapse of all the ages*. And we are enabled to apprehend at all what is sublime and noble only by the perpetual instilling and drenching of the reality that surrounds us [...] Let us spend our lives in conceiving then. The poet or the artist never yet had so fair and noble a design. (*Walden* 2.21, emphases added).

Both Eliot and Thoreau are saying "that God is both now and always and can only be glimpsed, much less 'apprehended,' through our constantly observing and seeking to absorb the reality around us, something that can only be done, to a certain extent, if a person actively stays still to absorb it" (43).

"chthonic" (223) – In, under, or beneath the earth, subterranean.

Commentary

Divination is a futile distraction since it concentrates upon the future. The "dimension" of past and future is linear time, but what matters is eternity and its link with human history, which is the Incarnation of Jesus Christ. Thus, while most people spend their lives looking back into the past or trying to gaze into the future, only the saint can "apprehend / The point of intersection of the timeless / With time" (200-202). The timeless is, of course, the dimension of eternality, while time is human time (chronology or duration). In contemplating the Incarnation, the saint is trying to grasp just this – the instant God became man, the intersection of the finite with the infinite. This sort of knowledge of time cannot be "an occupation" (202), such as most of us have. It is a perception that can only be given to those who have dedicated themselves to a life of "Ardour and selflessness and self-surrender," living their lives on a spiritual level (205).

Most of us simply get a momentary glimpse of the eternal, "the moment in and out of time" (207). This occurs when our minds are "unattended" (206), momentarily open to distraction from the day-to-day world so that we become "lost in a shaft of sunlight" (208) or "or music heard so deeply / That it is not heard at all" (210-211). This is what the speaker experienced in the garden of Burnt Norton. There was no music, or laughter of children in the shrubbery, or water in the pool except that he was the music, the laughter, and the water. It lasted only as long as he managed to keep it alive. This is not the experience of the saint, but it is something more than daytime consciousness.

Such moments afford only "hints and guesses" (212). Deborah Leiter explains:

> Saints may ultimately be able to apprehend the still point, he
> says, but he humbly admits that he's part of the other group, the
> "most of us," the majority of humans that only have occasional
> moments of illumination on their journeys. Then again, for
> Eliot, faith is more in the attempt than in the results […] (67)

People experience these transcendent moments in time, but they "miss the meaning" and fail to see how they point to a deeper reality and pattern of life. That can only be discovered through "prayer, observance, discipline, thought and action" (214). The "gift half understood, is Incarnation" (215): in the spirit made flesh in Jesus Christ, we have "the impossible union" – the eternal/mortal, the God/man (216).

In *The Rock* (1934), Eliot defined the Incarnation thus:

> Then came, at a predetermined moment, *a moment in time and*
> *of time,*
> A moment not out of time, but in time, in what we call history:
> transecting, bisecting the

world of time, *a moment in time but not like a moment of time*,
A moment in time but time was made through that moment: for
without the meaning there is no time, and that moment of time
gave the meaning.
Then it seemed as if men must proceed from light to light, in
the light of the Word,
*Through the Passion and Sacrifice saved in spite of their
negative being*;
Bestial as always before, carnal, self-seeking as always before,
selfish and purblind as ever before,
Yet always struggling, always reaffirming, always resuming
their march on the way that
was lit by the light;
Often halting, loitering, straying, delaying, returning, yet
following no other way.

Christ, who was God and man, in himself conquers and reconciles past and future
because the Incarnation *is* the Still Point, where the divine fills the human, where
the timeless manifests itself within time. Even our best attempts to understand it
are bound to fail because it defies language. But we are called to "work out our
salvation" nonetheless, for salvation is a process, part work, and part a gift of
God.

Without understanding the Incarnation, the narrator tells us that action is
simply movement because it does not have proper motivation. This kind of
movement characterizes a world enslaved to time, where everyone seems to be
driven by demons. In contrast, the "right action" (224) brings freedom from the
past and future by understanding Christ as the Still Point where "the past and
future / Are conquered, and reconciled" (218-219). That, incidentally, would
seem to indicate that the speculation that opened *Burnt Norton* was false. All time
is *not* "unredeemable" (5) because as well as the dimension of chronological time
(past, present, and future), there is also eternity. Unfortunately, "For most of us,
[grasping] this is the aim / Never here to be realized; / Who are only undefeated
/ Because we have gone on trying" (226-229). We will never fully comprehend
the great paradox, but Christ promises us resurrection, and we have to go on
trying to grasp that.

The yew tree that stands in the church graveyard, its roots reaching down to
the dead, is a sign of the resurrection. Now we can revert to our "temporal" world
(231), "content at the last" (230) in the knowledge that life is made significant
by eternity, not rendered absurd by it.

Summary of Part V

The speaker reviews the various ways people try to predict the future or reach
back into the past. Saints, however, experience the timeless dimension within the

dimension of time by perceiving the Still Point. Most people experience these transcendent moments in their lives, but they miss the meaning of these experiences. At most, they sense that such glimpses point to a deeper reality and pattern of life. The ultimate such experience is to grasp the paradox of the Incarnation of Christ where past and future are conquered and reconciled. The Incarnation is the Still Point, where the divine intersects with the human, where the timeless takes up residence within time. This is impossible for humans to understand; they can only keep trying to do so.

The speaker describes the hectic, indeed demonic, rush and action characterized by a world enslaved to linear time where there is only random, purposeless movement. In contrast, there is the "right action" of being still to contemplate Christ as the Still Point. Paradoxically, by so doing, we manage to live our lives in the world with greater content.

LITTLE GIDDING (1942)

Preparing to Read

1. What is the oldest human-made structure you have ever visited? A castle, a plantation house, the remains of an ancient city, the pyramids, the Great Serpent Mound in Ohio? What feelings did your visit prompt?

2. Have you ever visited a place with a history that you knew well? Jamestown, the Alamo, Gettysburg, the Houses of Parliament, Versailles? How did knowing the history of this place affect your experience of it?

3. Have you ever visited a particularly holy place? An ancient temple, a shrine, a church, a mosque, a monastery? How did the holiness of the place affect the way you felt as you looked around?

4. Is there one place that you would really like to go that you have not yet seen? What is it and why do you want to go there?

Part I Lines 1-20: "Midwinter spring is … Zero summer?"

Notes

"Sempiternal" (2) – Timeless, forever, eternal, never-ending, everlasting, endless, having beginning, but no end.

"brazier " (9) – A metal container used to burn solid fuel, including garden waste.

"pentecostal fire" (10) – Pentecost is a holy day that commemorates the descent of the Holy Spirit upon the followers of the crucified Christ and their speaking in foreign tongues. During the celebration of Pentecost in Jerusalem, the disciples received the Holy Spirit:

> And when the day of Pentecost was fully come, they were all with one accord in one place. And suddenly there came a sound from heaven as of a rushing mighty wind, and it filled all the house where they were sitting. And there appeared unto them cloven tongues like as of fire, and it sat upon each of them. And *they were all filled with the Holy Ghost, and began to speak with other tongues, as the Spirit gave them utterance.* And there were dwelling at Jerusalem Jews, devout men, out of every nation under heaven. Now when this was noised abroad, the multitude came together, and were confounded, because that every man heard them speak in his own language. And they were all amazed and marvelled, saying one to another, Behold, are not all these which speak Galilaeans? And how hear we every man in our own tongue, wherein we were born? Parthians, and Medes, and Elamites, and the dwellers in Mesopotamia, and in Judaea, and Cappadocia, in Pontus, and

115

Asia, Phrygia, and Pamphylia, in Egypt, and in the parts of Libya about Cyrene, and strangers of Rome, Jews and proselytes, Cretes and Arabians, we do hear them speak in our tongues the wonderful works of God. And they were all amazed, and were in doubt, saying one to another, What meaneth this? Others mocking said, These men are full of new wine. But Peter, standing up with the eleven, lifted up his voice, and said unto them, Ye men of Judaea, and all ye that dwell at Jerusalem, be this known unto you, and hearken to my words: For these are not drunken, as ye suppose, seeing it is but the third hour of the day. But this is that which was spoken by the prophet Joel; And it shall come to pass in the last days, saith God, I will pour out of my Spirit upon all flesh: and your sons and your daughters shall prophesy, and your young men shall see visions, and your old men shall dream dreams: And on my servants and on my handmaidens I will pour out in those days of my Spirit; and they shall prophesy: And I will shew wonders in heaven above, and signs in the earth beneath; blood, and fire, and vapour of smoke: The sun shall be turned into darkness, and the moon into blood, before the great and notable day of the Lord come: And it shall come to pass, that whosoever shall call on the name of the Lord shall be saved. Ye men of Israel, hear these words; Jesus of Nazareth, a man approved of God among you by miracles and wonders and signs, which God did by him in the midst of you, as ye yourselves also know: Him, being delivered by the determinate counsel and foreknowledge of God, ye have taken, and by wicked hands have crucified and slain: Whom God hath raised up, having loosed the pains of death: because it was not possible that he should be holden of it. For David speaketh concerning him, I foresaw the Lord always before my face, for he is on my right hand, that I should not be moved: Therefore did my heart rejoice, and my tongue was glad; moreover also my flesh shall rest in hope: Because thou wilt not leave my soul in hell, neither wilt thou suffer thine Holy One to see corruption [...] (*Acts* 2:1-27, KJV)

Pentecostalism emphasizes the direct personal experience of God through baptism with the Holy Spirit. "covenant" (14) – A formal, solemn, and binding agreement or compact. *Genesis* 9:8-11 records God's covenant with Noah and his descendants after the Flood, which destroyed the world. God promised that He would never again send a worldwide flood to destroy the earth as an act of His divine judgment for sin. God sealed the Noahic Covenant by forming a rainbow in the sky.

Commentary

Nasrulla Mambrol defines the progress that *Little Gidding* makes in the narrator's pursuit of the still moment, the moment in and out of time, "Rather than waiting for the unattended moment, which may never come or, coming, may be missed, the speaker opens himself up at Little Gidding, a space where 'prayer has been valid,' to this 'intersection of the timeless moment' that is 'England and nowhere. Never and always' […] the core thematic idea of 'The Four Quartets' […] is to find the complete conjunction of the personal, the historical, and the particular with the timeless and eternal" (op. cit).

The narrator describes an early afternoon on the shortest day of the year, the winter solstice. The day itself is a paradox: the sun shines so strongly in the middle of winter that it looks and feels like a day in spring. It is an anomaly: a spring day occurring in the middle of winter. The impact can be understood by comparison with e.e.cummings' poem "Chansons Innocentes: I":

> in Just-
> spring   when the world is mud-
> luscious the little
>
> …
>
> when the world is puddle-wonderful

To be clear, Cummings is describing something a little different – the earliest appearance of spring near the end of winter. However, his description of the vitalizing experience of spring helps the reader of *Little Gidding* to understand the speaker's sense of wonder at the paradox he is experiencing. Midwinter suggests the death of nature, but this day attests to the coming spring and the renewal of life. The springlike weather gives the impression of being endless (though the reality is that it will be fleeting); similarly, the narrator has the impression of being "Suspended in time" – a moment both in and out of time (3). Likewise, Little Gidding is suspended "between pole and tropic" since England is located in the temperate latitudes where the change of seasons is clearly marked. But here, that cycle of the year appears to be suspended. The whole description seems to be an extended metaphor for the moment of spiritual understanding and faith that comes in the deepest dark night of the soul.

Everything is frozen and dead, yet blazing with the sun reflecting off the frozen water of the "pond and ditches" (5), linking two burning elements of "frost and fire" (4). This recalls the incident of the sun shining on the empty pool at Burnt Norton, which suddenly appeared full, but the difference is that, on that occasion, the sun produced an illusion that the pool was full. Here there is no illusion. The glare temporarily blinds the speaker. Another anomaly is that the "windless cold […] is the heart's heat" (6), by which I take it he means that though the day is cold, what he is experiencing literally warms his heart – it is inspiring. Perhaps the speaker means that the inner warmth of spiritual understanding can kick in only when life gets close to death.

More paradox follows. The "glow" of the spirit is actually more intense than would be the physical "blaze of branch, or brazier" (9). All of these lines use heavy alliteration to push home their point. What is happening to the speaker is a stirring of "the dumb spirit" not with the physical wind "but pentecostal fire" (10), a message of eternal hope such as the apostles received when they were in the depths of despair over the crucifixion of Christ. The Christian holiday of Pentecost (called 'White Sunday' or 'Whitsunday' or 'Whitsun' in the U.K.) is celebrated on the fiftieth day (the seventh Sunday) from Easter Sunday, so it is in spring. That spring day had spontaneously appeared at Little Gidding.

This moment of spiritual insight takes place in time, "Between melting and freezing" (11), but it is not *of* time because "There is no earth smell / Or smell of living thing" (12-13). This is a quickening of the "soul's sap" (12), not the sap of the winter plants, so this is "the spring time" that is "not in time's covenant" (14). In contrast to the dancing in *East Coker*, this, as Stephen Spender explains, "is the intersection of a moment in time with eternity" (Eliot, 162). It is "[the] experience of intersection between God's time and your time [...] a moment of insight when an image or experience suddenly deepens your understanding of the sacred story, as we live and tell it in this particular season. And you really must wait for it; these things can't be forced" (Gina N. Brown, "Intersection of Time And Eternality." Oct. 9, 2019. Web. Nov. 24, 2021).

So this is a "spring time" that is "not in time's covenant" because it is a springtime of the soul. The narrator returns to describing the natural world about him. The hedgerow that would be white with flowers in the spring, today it is blooming with snow – a bloom that comes and goes suddenly, unlike the spring bloom that first buds and then slowly fades. So this blossoming is "Not in the scheme of generation" (18). It has nothing to do with physical regeneration or the coming of summer. Physical summer, at this moment of mid-winter, is "unimaginable" (19). Thus, while the natural world is emblematic of this spiritual possibility, they are not the same. One is transient, and the other is eternal. This naturally prompts the question, "Where is the summer, the unimaginable / Zero summer?" This summer symbolizes the permanent state of being at once inside and outside of time. That would be a state of endless bliss. But how is it to be attained? That is the question to which the narrator turns.

All this talk of the white blossom of spring buds on the trees and the white blossom of winter snow on the trees puts me in mind of a beautiful poem by A. E. Housman:

> Loveliest of trees, the cherry now
> Is hung with bloom along the bough,
> And stands about the woodland ride
> Wearing white for Eastertide.
>
> Now, of my threescore years and ten,

Twenty will not come again,
And take from seventy springs a score,
It only leaves me fifty more.

And since to look at things in bloom
Fifty springs are little room,
About the woodlands I will go
To see the cherry hung with snow.

Having reread the Housman poem in the light of *Four Quartets*, it seems to me that the essential spiritual message is similar.

Part I Lines 20 -39: "If you came this way … Now and in England."

Notes

"broken king" (26) – King Charles I visited the manor of Little Gidding three times, including when he sought refuge there after the Royalist defeat at the Battle of Naseby, which ultimately led to his capture and execution.

Commentary

The speaker describes the spiritual path. He addresses the reader directly, speculating on how the reader might approach the church at Little Gidding. In spring, the route followed would be precisely the same as that he has followed, and the hedges would be white as they are now but with blossom, not snow. One would approach surrounded by the "voluptuary sweetness" (24) of natural growth and flowers, but the result would be the same as the narrator has reached. If one came at night like a defeated, "broken king" (as the fugitive Charles I did in May 1645) or by day quite by chance "not knowing what you came for" (30), the end result would be the same. You would have to leave the "rough road" (28), which presumably symbolizes the life we usually lead that is full of actions and plans and business, and pass the "pig-sty" (29), which may represent all of the 'stuff' that clutters up our lives, to get to "the dull façade [of the medieval parish church of St. John] / And the tombstone" (29-30). These do not in themselves sound particularly inspiring, but they would bring you face to face with your own headstone – your own mortality.

A person comes to Little Gidding either with no conscious purpose at all (perhaps they are just out for a walk in the country) or with some definite purpose (to take a photograph or simply to see the church and the graveyard). If the latter, the purpose was only "a husk of meaning" (31) which disintegrates as soon as it is achieved – we are left with no lasting achievement. In either case, however, a deeper purpose emerges that is "beyond the end you figured / And is altered in fulfilment" (33-34). That is, the ostensible reason for coming is transformed and deepened by what one experiences there. Nor is Little Gidding the only place where such a spiritual revelation is possible. Others are spread out around the world, at "the world's end, some at the sea jaws, / Or over a dark lake, in a desert or a city—" but this is the closest, and it is in England (36-37).

Deborah Leiter explains:

> The speaker here points out that the eternal transcends seasonality and time itself; a human being is clearly within time and within specific instances and at specific places on earth when one is approaching the "intersection of the timeless moment" (LG 52), but at the "still point" itself, the human steps out of time temporarily into the eternal, so a particular season or time of day doesn't matter when approaching a place where the timeless intersects with time. From that vantage point the human experiencing the "timeless moment" can see time and the dance performed within it more clearly. (69)

So, the speaker seems to believe that there are certain sites around the world where it is easier to gain hints and guesses at spiritual truth.

Part I Lines 39-53: "If you came ... Never and always."

"the intersection of the timeless moment" (52) – What Eliot is describing is clearly related to the thought of William Blake (1757-1827). I was particularly pleased to find the following clear account of Blake's beliefs by Larry Clayton:

> Blake used Six Thousand years to represent the Time that had elapsed since creation. Before creation there was no time, only Eternity. The six thousand year period as it relates to Eternity is a moment where there is the appearance of occurrences outside of Eternity. In Time "all things vanish and are seen no more." In Eternity the productions of Time leave "lineaments permanent for ever & ever."
>
> To Blake inspiration occurs at the intersection between Time and Eternity. The moment of inspiration seems to have no duration because it moves outside of Time and within Eternity. We may create the image of an exchange between Time and Eternity at these pregnant points which allows a flow in either or both directions. We may invite Eternity into the Time through which we are flowing, or we may exit Time and leave behind its restraints to enjoy the expanded perception of Eternity. ("William Blake: Religion and Psychology." Jan. 6, 2020. Web. Nov. 24, 2021)

Commentary

To come "this way" is not, of course, literally to come to Little Gidding but to take the spiritual path. That path will be the same no matter what one's starting point, route, or the time of year. The journey requires a putting off of one's worldly senses. You do not come here "verify" (43) some fact about the place or learn something or just satisfy idle curiosity, or to have a good story to tell when one returns. Those are every day, touristy motives. You come to pray, "to kneel / Where prayer has been valid" (45-46). This is a place where others have prayed whose prayers have been answered. Prayer is more than reciting "an order of words" (47), more than merely being conscious that we are praying, and more than the "sound of the voice praying" (48). These, as Hamlet would say, "are actions that a man might play; But I have that within which passeth show" (*Hamlet* 1,2).

What the dead in the churchyard had not the capacity to put into words when they were alive, being dead, they can communicate. They do not, of course, communicate in language. The communication is of the spiritual kind that the apostles experienced at Pentecost, "tongued with fire beyond the language of the living" (51). One has come to a place where the living and the dead communicate, where mortals come face to face with eternity, creating "the timeless moment" that occurs in time (52). This junction of past, present and future with eternity is not simply the function of a chance memory; it is a glimpse of the truth that passeth understanding.

The section ends, "Here, the intersection of the timeless moment / Is England and nowhere. Never and always" (52-53). This is more paradox, as though the narrator is trying to get the reader to acknowledge that he/she cannot actually understand such a moment – it must be experienced. B. Rajan explains, "Little Gidding is a poem about history, history felt as real in one's bones, a vitality drawn from the power of the past which liberates one for action in the present" ("The Unity of the Quartets" in Rajan Ed. 91).

Summary of Part I

The narrator describes a visit to the chapel at Little Gidding in the middle of winter. The weather is unseasonably warm and spring-like. He uses the oxymoron "Midwinter spring" to describe this paradox. It is season unto itself, containing both the frost of winter (i.e., the past) and the warmth of the spring sun (i.e., the future). Ironically, he notes that if you came to the churchyard on a day in May, the hedges would be similarly white, not with snow (i.e., the present) but with blossom (i.e., the future). If you came at night, the flowers in bloom would still be the same, the only difference being the intention and purpose of the visitor. Both the traveler by day and the traveler by night arrive at the same place, regardless of their purposes.

Arrival at the garden in the churchyard is a metaphor for attaining the Still Point, the intersection of the timeless moment within time. To be ready for this experience requires the renunciation of one's desires, humility, and constant prayer. It is not to be analyzed or verified. The new life of the Spirit comes only when one has renounced the self, the individual ego.

Study Guide

Part II Lines 54-77: "Ash on an old man's sleeve ... of water and fire."

Notes

"Ash on an old man's sleeve" (54) – Nasrulla Mambrol explains:

> The ash that falls "on an old man's sleeve" as the second section begins is clearly the soot and dust in the air from London's nightly fires in the present moment as the city endures the constant German air attacks. Where there was a house and the lives lived in it, there now is nothing. "This," the speaker tells us, like a bell tolling the final hour, "is the death of air." The litany of doom and terror continues as in each succeeding stanza the speaker makes the reader painfully mindful of the tragedies unfolding all around him. Existence collapses into its absence, which is death. (op. cit.)

"drouth" (62) – A rather old-fashioned spelling of drought.

"eviscerated" (66) – To eviscerate is to remove the internal organs from a body. Eviscerated soil would be inorganic, sterile, and lacking fertility.

"the vanity of toil" (67) – Inevitably, one thinks of "Ozymandias" (1818) by Percy Shelley (1792-822):

> I met a traveller from an antique land,
> Who said – "Two vast and trunkless legs of stone
> Stand in the desert. ... Near them, on the sand,
> Half sunk a shattered visage lies, whose frown,
> And wrinkled lip, and sneer of cold command,
> Tell that its sculptor well those passions read
> Which yet survive, stamped on these lifeless things,
> The hand that mocked them, and the heart that fed;
> And on the pedestal, these words appear:
> "My name is Ozymandias, King of Kings;
> Look on my Works, ye Mighty, and despair!"
> Nothing beside remains. Round the decay
> Of that colossal Wreck, boundless and bare
> The lone and level sands stretch far away.

Commentary

The next three stanzas deal with the death of the four elements – air, earth, water, and fire. In the first, the air is full of dust, and this dust is all that remains of the past. The burnt roses leave only "Ash on an old man's sleeve" (54). Inevitably, this recalls the roses in *Burnt Norton*. There they were associated with past happiness and perhaps with a love affair that ended long ago (for which roses would be very appropriate). Now withered and dry, those roses could be recovered by memory, but burned roses are beyond recovery. The dust he

122

breathes in "was a house" (58). This also could be the dust of the manor house that burnt down and was never rebuilt. It could also refer to the burned landscape of London destroyed by German bombing raids during the Second World War. The dust still hangs heavy in the air so that people breathe it in. They are literally inhaling death, bringing "The death of hope and despair" (60) to those who live on – those who have survived love affairs and bombing.

The earth itself is dead: either drowned by floods or parched by drought. Since we inhabit the earth, we are submerged as either the water or the sand level rises "Over the eyes and in the mouth" (63). Both the water and the soil are dead. The soil exposed by the fallen, ruined buildings "Gapes at the vanity of toil, / Laughs without mirth" (67-68). They are mocking humanity's feeble attempts to build something that will last. Perhaps Eliot is drawing on his personal experience of emerging from the air raid shelters and breathing in the dust raised by the night's bombing. In such a landscape, all of our efforts to make meaning of our lives seem vain and pointless. The very earth laughs at "the vanity of toil" (67).

Between them, water and fire destroy everything: town, pasture, weed. Nothing but them remains. They are forces of nature whose strength mocks every attempt by man to construct something meaningful on earth. They also "deride / The sacrifice that we denied" (72-73). This seems to reference Christ's sacrifice on the cross, which was made to give man eternal life but which modern people no longer have faith in. It might also be a reference to the sacrifices made by previous generations that modern people have similarly forgotten. Either way, religious buildings (like that at Little Gidding) are not immune, "Water and fire shall rot / The marred foundations we forgot, / Of sanctuary and choir" (76-77). The narrator sees the destruction he has described as a result of modern man's loss of faith. If humanity chooses to exist only in chronological time, then humans can only be defeated by the passage of time.

Part II Lines 78 – 96: "In the uncertain ... intimate and unidentifiable."

Notes

"dusk" (91) – This word is usually associated with the gathering darkness of evening, but it is equally used to describe the lifting darkness around dawn.

Commentary

The second half of Part II moves into an Anglicized version of the Italian *terza rima* form. This and the general tone of dark despair recall the early Renaissance Florentine poet Dante Alighieri. In his essay "What Dante Means to Me" (1950), Eliot said this passage was "the nearest equivalent to a canto of the *Inferno* or the *Purgatorio* [the first and second parts of the three-part *Divine Comedy*], in style as well as content, that I could achieve [... in order] to present to the mind of the reader a parallel between the *Inferno* and the *Purgatorio,* which

Dante visited, and a hallucinated scene after an air-raid."

The narrator describes predawn in war-torn London. Early in the war, the Germans had discovered that daytime raids of the capital city proved too costly in terms of planes shot down and had switched to nighttime raids. Eliot is drawing on his own experience as a fire watcher on the roof of his employer's publishing firm, the publishers Faber and Faber, during the Luftwaffe bombing raids. That would certainly explain why dawn comes after what has appeared to be an "interminable" night (79). The narrator repeats this idea but with a paradox: dawn always comes as "the recurrent end of the unending." This could be a reference to the apparently unending bombing of London. The dawn has ended this raid, but there will be another the next night, and on and on. More importantly, although dawn always comes to end the night, metaphorically speaking, spiritual enlightenment comes to relieve the darkest night of the soul.

The "dark dove" is an oxymoron since doves are usually white and represent peace while this dove finds its way home in a time of war. The phrase "flickering tongue" (81) suggests that the narrator refers to the German aircraft that have passed below the horizon and are on their way home. Perhaps the dove represents the narrator's night fears because fire watching during a bombing raid must have been a pretty scary experience. The only sound is "the dead leaves [which] still rattled on like tin" (83) in the deserted streets "where no sound was" (84). In this context, "still' means 'constantly' or 'endlessly.' The dead leaves are perhaps symbolic of the victims of the air raid and the destruction caused, both of which the bomber leaves behind.

The narrator has emerged into the city, "Between three districts whence the smoke arose" (85). He is surrounded at a distance by the death and destruction that he has escaped. At this point, he encounters a man whose progress toward him is like that of the leaves blown intermittently by the wind, "walking, loitering and hurried" (86). This is how leaves move, rapidly when there is a gust of wind and slowly or not at all when the wind falls. The man appears to have no agency of his own; he is simply pushed "Before the urban dawn wind unresisting" (88).

Part II Lines 97 - 144: "So I assume ... blowing of the horn."

Notes

"'What are *you* here?'" (98) – The figure was originally addressed in the poem as "Ser Brunetto" before being revised to the ambiguous pronoun "you." In a letter to John Hayward (August 27, 1942), Eliot sought to explain this revision:

> I think you will recognise that it was necessary to get rid of
> Brunetto for two reasons. The first is that the visionary figure
> has now become somewhat more definite and will no doubt be
> identified by some readers with Yeats though I do not mean
> anything so precise as that. However, I do not wish to take the
> responsibility of putting Yeats or anybody else into Hell and I

do not want to impute to him the particular vice which took Brunetto there. Secondly, although the reference to that Canto is intended to be explicit, I wish the effect of the whole to be Purgatorial which is more appropriate. That brings us to the reference to swimming in fire which you will remember at the end of Purgatorio 26 where the poets are found.

"peregrine" (121) – Having a tendency to wander.

Commentary

Critics inform us that Eliot's model for this section is an episode from Dante's *Inferno* in which the poet meets Brunetto Latini (c.1220–1294), the Italian philosopher and statesman who was Dante's guardian after the death of his father. The two meet in the third ring of the Seventh Circle, the Circle of the Violent against God. A great deal of ink has been expended in trying to identify the being whom the speaker meets. Is it Shelley, Yeats, or Dante himself? Could it be the poet's old friend and mentor, Ezra Pound, identified by the comic pun in the phrase "a familiar com*pound* ghost" (95)? Is Eliot referring to his own and Pound's anti-Semitic statements (which in Pound's case had led him to choose the German/Italian side in the war) and the resulting Holocaust when he writes of "things ill done and done to others' harm" (141)?

Perhaps, it is more fruitful to look closely at what the narrator says about the stranger he encounters. The man looks down toward the ground, pointedly not looking at the speaker. This is unusual, for it is almost automatic to look closely at the first person we encounter at dawn, as the speaker points out. That certainly is what the narrator is doing, fixing upon the man, "That pointed scrutiny with which we challenge / The first-met stranger in the waning dusk" (90-91). The speaker realizes with something of a shock that he is looking at, "some dead master / Whom I had known, forgotten, half recalled" (92-93). This certainly suggests that the entity is someone who taught the narrator his craft, whether literally or figuratively. The person's "brown baked features" (94) certainly suggest Dante tanned by the Italian sun. But then the speaker realizes that the figure is not one master but "Both one and many [...] a familiar compound ghost" (94-95). This leads to more paradoxes because the figure is at once "Both intimate and unidentifiable" (96). In one way, this is easily understood. All readers will have had the experience of meeting someone whom they know that they know but being unable to recall a name or even how they know the person. However, being a composite figure suggests that the speaker cannot identify the figure because it does not have a single identity. Perhaps he represents the poetic tradition in which Eliot was raised, making him a composite figure of all the masters who have gone before.

The two are approaching each other on the bombed city street with no one else around. The narrator cannot just ignore the figure (very impolite and unBritish!), so he "assumed a double part" (97) and responds to the figure as Dante did to his poetic master Brunetto Latino in the circle of the Sodomites, "'What! are *you* here?'" (98). By "assumed a double part," I think he means that he pretended to recognize the person; that is, he played the part of recognizing an old friend even though, in reality, he still could not identify the person. That is why the narrator hears "another's voice" (98) shouting out the greeting.

More paradox! The words, "'What! are *you* here?'" are enough to "compel the recognition they preceded" (102). By shouting a greeting that should have resulted from recognition, the narrator compels himself to recognize the stranger. Once again, this is on one level perfectly intelligible: we meet someone we cannot quite place and engaging him in conversation prompts our memory. Anyway, it works for the speaker: the two walk on together as the wind blows them, treading "the pavement in a dead patrol" (107). Their patrol is dead in the obvious sense that the bombing raid is over, and the patrols have ended since they have no purpose. In another sense, both of the companions are dead because they are, "'In concord at this intersection time / Of meeting nowhere, no before and after" (105-106). The two meet in a timeless moment unconnected with either past or future because the meeting is entirely unexpected and fortuitous, and it will have no sequel. Once they part, that will be the end of it.

The narrator addresses his companion determined to get him to speak. He says, "'The wonder that I feel is easy, / Yet ease is cause of wonder. Therefore speak: / I may not comprehend, may not remember'" (108-110). The narrator is seeking some wisdom. He does not want this opportunity to pass without having learned something of value. The wording here is nothing like colloquial English. It all seems very artificial and stilted, as though Eliot might have plucked the lines out of Dante. The theme, however, is familiar: human knowledge cannot be passed on effectively from one person or generation to the next. In life, everything is always in a state of flux.

The dead master insists that he has not come to recount his old "'thoughts and theory'" (112) that the narrator once knew and has since forgotten. Old ideas, even the narrator's own, belong in the past; they are done with. All we can do is to "'pray they [our ideas will] be forgiven'" (114) by the people who were influenced by them. Perhaps strangely, this applies to both the "'bad and good'" (116) thoughts and theories that we had. Again, the reader will understand this: we have all said things in the past, perhaps with the best intentions, that ended up being wrong and even hurtful. Even the things we said that might have been right may have become irrelevant, even harmful, with the passage of time.

The anonymous speaker insists what is past is past. "'Last season's fruit is eaten,'" and it cannot be eaten again (116). The figure uses a rather comic image of a fully-fed animal kicking over the useless empty bucket that contained its food. He tells the narrator, "'last year's words belong to last year's language / And next year's words await another voice'" (118-119). This, of course, echoes what the narrator said about writing in *East Coker*:

> [...] and every attempt
> Is a wholly new start, and a different kind of failure
> Because one has only learnt to get the better of words
> For the thing one no longer has to say, or the way in which
> One is no longer disposed to say it. (148-152)

The challenge for the writer is to constantly create a new language and a new voice. This recalls Ezra Pound's modernist credo, "Make It New," in his 1934 collection of essays of the same name, calling upon writers to create out of the tradition of art, work that is distinctively innovative. There are, however, limits. The artist must finally pass the torch to "another voice."

Being a spirit, the dead master finds now that he can make the "'passage'" between the world of the past and the present (the dead and the living) without "'hindrance'" (120) and that he is able to find "'words I never thought to speak / In streets I never thought I should revisit'" when he died in a foreign country (123-124). He feels like the worlds of spirit and everyday life have "'become much like each other'" (122) and finds he has things to say that he had never thought of before in words he had not thought to use. On the one hand, this implies that the individual consciousness does not disappear with death, but on the other, there is something frustrating about this new wisdom since it cannot be communicated – except as now in a chance encounter with the like-minded narrator. The master states that their joint endeavor was constantly "'To purify the dialect of the tribe'" (127) and in so doing to "'urge the mind to aftersight and foresight'" (128). As writers, they tried to make the language more precise. They tried to take the reader to a place where past and future are part of time present.

This being the purpose of the poet, the figure says he will "'disclose the gifts reserved for age / To set a crown upon your lifetime's effort'" (129-130). This suggests some sort of climax to the writer's career (something like the Nobel Prize in Literature, for example). Still, it is yet to be seen whether the master is speaking seriously or ironically.

According to the stranger, the "gifts reserved for age" are the loss of the five senses, the powerless of an old person's rage at the folly of his fellows, and the shame of past actions, past motives and past wrongs done to others. We experience the world through our senses, but as we age, these become less receptive to stimuli from the outside world, "'As body and soul begin to fall asunder'" (134). As we age, we feel anger at "human folly" (136), about which we know ourselves to be impotent because we can change nothing. Thus, we can only laugh at man's follies, but that laughter is no longer amusing; it tears and rips at our heart and mind. Finally, we relive our actions, feel the shame of what motivated us to act as we did, and experience again, "'things ill done and done to others' harm / Which once you took for exercise of virtue'" (141-142). When we understand our failures, the approval we get from fools "'stings'" our conscience and the honor we receive feels like a stain.

The figure describes a spirit trapped in purgatory, constantly going "'From wrong to wrong'" (144), trapped in a cycle of guilt and self-recrimination. However, there is the possibility of restoration "'by the refining fire / Where you must move in measure, like a dancer'" (145-146). The refining fire is a reference back to Pentecost, which is the promise of eternal life to mortal men where we "must move in measure, like a dancer." There, it is implied, guilt for one's sins will be purged away. There we shall engage in a dynamic movement without progression.

With that rather ambiguous blessing, the figure takes its leave as the day breaks in the streets broken and disfigured by bombs. It is, the narrator knows, "a kind of valediction" (143), but its significance is yet to appear in the poem. Perhaps the "blowing of the horn" (144) is the sounding of the all-clear after the air-raid.

Summary of Part II

The narrator, conscious that his advancing years bring him closer to death, is also aware that the war threatens the end of civilization itself. The speaker describes encountering a mysterious figure at dawn in London during the Blitz. The anonymous stranger appears to represent all of the writers who have gone before. He, like the narrator, has wrestled with language to communicate what he learned about the past and future. Now, however, he counsels that human wisdom is merely temporal. At best, it will soon be forgotten; at worst, it will be seen in hindsight to have hurt and harmed.

The stranger offers to share the wisdom he has learned and by telling the narrator about "'the gifts reserved for age / To set a crown upon your lifetime's effort'" (129-130). Although not immediately evident, the tone here is bitterly ironic – even cynical. Old age brings physical decrepitude, awareness of one's powerlessness, and regret for the errors of one's past – a reality that makes a mockery of the respect that people show to old men. Clinging to the self even after death means existing in a cycle of misery. Only by the death of the self and the acceptance of the refining and redeeming power of the Holy Spirit can one enter the Still Point where one moves "'in measure, like a dancer'" (151).

Part III Lines 145-160: "There are three conditions ... in another pattern."

Commentary

The third section describes the three stages of spiritual growth. These "often look alike / Yet differ completely" (155-156), like three different plants flowering in the same hedgerow. The first is attachment to the self and things and people; that is, living on the material plane in the everyday world – developing one's ego, earning money to accumulate material goods, and interacting with other people. The second is detachment *from* the self and things and people – seeking to avoid the material plane of life, as monks and nuns do. These ways are, respectively, the ways of life and death-in-life – embracing life within linear time and trying to avoid it. "[G]rowing between" these two extremes, and resembling them "as death resembles life" is the third way: "indifference" (148-140).

This means neither attachment to nor detachment from temporal and material things. It means devotion to that which is spiritual and eternal. The third way involves "the use of the memory" (151) to generate a "love beyond desire" (153). The idea here seems to be that if I love something that exists purely in my memory, I really cannot get caught up in wanting to possess it – as I should if I were to fall in love with someone in the present. The narrator is here describing agape love, the kind of love that involves a choice to put another's interests above our own; it is unselfish, giving (even to the point of self-sacrifice), and unconditional. Such is the love that God feels for all his creation. Thus, the third way is "liberation / From the future as well as the past" (153-154). It has neither past nor future; it is always now.

All of this is rather abstract and theoretical, so the speaker gives an example. Love of country begins in patriotism and nationalism, both of which dictate certain forms of action (perhaps waving a flag, or joining a parade, or going to war). However, true love of country "comes to find that action of little importance" (156). Thus, history may produce "servitude" (157) initially, but later it can "be freedom" (158). So "faces and places, [disappear] with the self" (159). We loved them as best we could with our human love, but now we love them in a way that allows them, and ourselves, to "become renewed, transfigured, in another pattern" (160). What this pattern is, the narrator does not say. It could simply be becoming part of the earth and continuing the recycling of atoms (since matter can neither be created nor destroyed); it could be becoming part of the cycle of the seasons; it could be God's promise of resurrection into eternal life.

Part III Lines 161-194: "Sin is Behovely … of our beseeching."

Notes

"Sin is Behovely, but / All shall be well, and / All manner of thing shall be well." (161-163) – 'Behovely' means necessary and useful. Thus the meaning is, "Sin was necessary (i.e., bound to happen), but it is going to be well, everything is going to be well." These ideas come from *Revelations of Divine Love*, written between the 14th and 15th centuries by Dame Julian of Norwich (1343-after 1416). Chapter 86 reads:

> And I saw full surely that ere God made us he loved us; which love was never lacking nor ever shall be. And in this love he has made all his works; and in this love he has made all things profitable to us; and in this love our life is everlasting [...] in

129

which love we have our beginning. And all this shall we see in God, without end.

The Thirteenth Revelation reads:

> After this the Lord brought to my mind the longing that I had to Him afore. And I saw that nothing letted me but sin. And so I looked, generally, upon us all, and methought: *If sin had not been, we should all have been clean and like to our Lord, as He made us.*
>
> And thus, in my folly, afore this time often I wondered why by the great foreseeing wisdom of God the beginning of sin was not letted: for then, methought, all should have been well. This stirring [of mind] was much to be forsaken, but nevertheless mourning and sorrow I made therefor, without reason and discretion.
>
> But Jesus, who in this Vision informed me of all that is needful to me, answered by this word and said: *It behoved that there should be sin; but all shall be well, and all shall be well, and all manner of thing shall be well.*
>
> In this naked word *sin*, our Lord brought to my mind, generally, *all that is not good*, and the shameful despite and the utter noughting that He bare for us in this life, and His dying; and all the pains and passions of all His creatures, ghostly and bodily; (for we be all partly noughted, and we shall be noughted following our Master, Jesus, till we be full purged, that is to say, till we be fully noughted of our deadly flesh and of all our inward affections which are not very good;) and the beholding of this, with all pains that ever were or ever shall be,—and with all these I understand the Passion of Christ for most pain, and overpassing. All this was shewed in a touch and quickly passed over into comfort: for our good Lord would not that the soul were affeared of this terrible sight.
>
> But I saw not *sin*: for I believe it hath no manner of substance nor no part of being, nor could it be known but by the pain it is cause of.
>
> And thus pain, *it* is something, as to my sight, for a time; for it purgeth, and maketh us to know ourselves and to ask mercy. For the Passion of our Lord is comfort to us against all this, and so is His blessed will. And for the tender love that our good Lord hath to all that shall be saved, He comforteth readily and sweetly, signifying thus: *It is sooth that sin is cause of all this pain; but all shall be well, and all shall be well, and all manner [of] thing shall be well.*

These words were said full tenderly, showing no manner of blame to me nor to any that shall be saved. Then were it a great unkindness to blame or wonder on God for my sin, since He blameth not me for sin.

And in these words I saw a marvellous high mystery hid in God, which mystery He shall openly make known to us in Heaven: in which knowing we shall verily see the cause why He suffered sin to come. In which sight we shall endlessly joy in our Lord God.

(Emphasis in original)

"By the purification of the motive / In the ground of our beseeching." (193-194) – From Dame Julian of Norwich, *Revelations of Divine Love*, The Fourteenth Revelation. There she writes:

Beseeching is a true, gracious, lasting will of the soul, oned and fastened into the will of our Lord by the sweet inward work of the Holy Ghost. Our Lord Himself, He is the first receiver of our prayer, as to my sight, and taketh it full thankfully and highly enjoying; and He sendeth it up above and setteth it in the Treasure, where it shall never perish. It is there afore God with all His Holy continually received, ever speeding [the help of] our needs; and when we shall receive our bliss it shall be given us for a degree of joy, with endless worshipful thanking from Him.

Full glad and merry is our Lord of our prayer; and He looketh thereafter and He willeth to have it because with His grace He maketh us like to Himself in condition as we are in kind: and so is His blissful will. Therefore He saith thus: *Pray inwardly, though thee thinketh it savour thee not: for it is profitable, though thou feel not, though thou see nought; yea, though thou think thou canst not. For in dryness and in barrenness, in sickness and in feebleness, then is thy prayer well-pleasant to me, though thee thinketh it savour thee nought but little. And so is all thy believing prayer in my sight.* For the meed and the endless thanks that He will give us, *therefor* He is covetous to have us pray continually in His sight. God accepteth the goodwill and the travail of His servant, howsoever we feel: wherefore it pleaseth Him that we work both in our prayers and in good living, by His help and His grace, reasonably with discretion keeping our powers [turned] to Him, till when that we have Him that we seek, in fulness of joy: that is, Jesus.

(Emphasis in original)

Commentary

The narrator quotes the medieval English mystic Julian (or Juliana) of Norwich, "Sin is Behovely, but / All shall be well, and / all manner of thing shall be well" (161-163). Although sin is an inevitable part of being human, it is also useful. Sin does not absolutely and finally banish humanity from the presence of God. It is not the end of the human story because there is a way to overcome one's sins and attain spiritual wholeness. The church at Little Gidding has, over the centuries, attracted people of all sorts, some "not wholly commendable, / Of no immediate kin or kindness" (165-166) and some of "peculiar genius" (167). Yet when they came there, they were "All touched by a common genius" (168). That is, everyone who came was inspired by the spirit of the place to be better. At the time, this very striving divided them between Anglo-Catholics and Puritans, yet the striving united them.

The narrator recalls King Charles I, head of the High Church Anglican Communion, who came to Little Gidding in the night and was later executed by Puritan Parliamentarians "on the scaffold" (171). The "three men" might refer to other executions during the English Civil War (1642-1651). For example, Archbishop of Canterbury William Laud (1573-1645), a supporter of Charles I's religious reforms, was arrested by Parliament in 1640 and executed in 1645. The line may also reference the death of Christ with a robber on each side. Others are mentioned who suffered the same fate or "died forgotten" (172). John Milton (1608-1674), the Puritan who opposed Charles, was "one who died blind and quiet" (174). Why should these dead men be celebrated more than those who are dying at this very moment in war? It is certainly not because we want to go back to their times or "revive old factions [... or] restore old policies" (180-181) that divided the country. Praying for them is not "an incantation / To summon the spectre of a Rose" (178-179). This seems to be a reference to a yet earlier civil war, in the mid-to-late fifteenth. The Wars of the Roses, a series of civil wars fought for the English crown in the mid-to-late fifteenth century, were so-called because a white rose symbolized the House of York, and a red rose the House of Lancaster

The speaker argues that we should have no wish to revive or restore those times or bring back those divisions because now these enemies, "Accept the constitution of silence / And are folded in a single party" (175-176). They are all dead and therefore united in spirit. From their defeat (their mortality), we inherit "a symbol: / A symbol perfected in death" (189-190) which assures us that all will be well when our motives, like theirs, have been purified, "In the ground of our beseeching" (194). What does this mean? It seems to mean that in our prayers, we should be humble. Like the dead, our motives should be indifferent to the world and to our particular participation in the world. The true prayer should be that uttered by Christ while he was in agony on the cross, "Father, if Thou be willing, remove this cup from Me: nevertheless not My will, but Thine, be done" (*Luke* 22:42, KJV).

Summary of Part III

The narrator examines three states which seem identical but are very different: attachment, detachment, and indifference to or from oneself, things, and people. Attachment and detachment are contrasting extremes, but indifference is the Still Point. It is the point in which memory brings liberation by creating timeless moments in time that transcend the moment in which they occur. Sin unites us all in a fellowship of the wounded, but in death, the purifying fires of the Spirit redeem us as they have those who went before. It is in the "ground" of death (both the sanctified 'portal' that is Little Gidding and the humility of acceptance) that we are purified of sin. It is here where our prayers of union with Christ are answered.

Part IV Lines 195-208: "The dove descending ... fire or fire."

Notes

"The dove descending" (195) – This inverts the imagery of George Meredith's "The Lark Ascending," which had been turned into the celebrated piece of music by Vaughan Williams. The second verse begins:

> For singing till his heaven fills,
> 'T is love of earth that he instils,
> And ever winging up and up,
> Our valley is his golden cup,
> And he the wine which overflows
> To lift us with him as he goes [...]

The dove is a Stukker dive bomber (the Junkers Ju 87) whose screaming descent was terrifying to those on the ground. According to the *Catholic Encyclopedia*, "The dove in flight is the symbol of the Ascension of Christ or of the entry into glory of the martyrs and saints" [... compare] 'Our soul is escaped as a bird from the snare of the hunters, the snare is broken and we are delivered' [*Psalms* 124:7, KJV]."

"intolerable shirt of flame" (205) – For attempting to rape his wife, Deianira, the centaur Nessus was slain by Herakles. However, before dying, Nessus had "convinced Deianira that the blood from his wound, if smeared on a garment, would act as a love potion on whoever wore the garment. Later, when Deianira was afraid that she was losing Herakles to another woman, she followed Nessus's advice, but he had tricked her, perhaps in order to gain a posthumous revenge on the hero. The blood-stained garment did not act as a love potion when the unwitting Herakles put it on, but instead as a poison that caused Herakles such unbearable agony that he was able to escape the pain only by lighting his own funeral pyre and then ascending to Olympus in the consuming flames" (Nasrullah Mambrol, op. cit.). A second possible source is Euripides' tragedy *Medea* in which, to gain revenge for her husband Jason's planned marriage to a Corinthian princess, Medea sends a poisoned robe as a wedding gift to his betrothed. The moment that it touches her skin, it burns off her flesh, and her father, King Creon, who rushes to save her, suffers the same fate the moment that he touches her. "Love is the unfamiliar Name" (203) – The inscription of Hell's Gate in Dante's *Inferno* reads (in Eliot's translation from his essay on Dante):

> Justice moved my high Maker
> What made me were the divine Power
> The supreme Wisdom, and the primal Love.

1 John states, "God is love" (4:16, KJV). This raises the paradox that the architect of all suffering both in this world and the next is a loving God. Since the operation of reason cannot understand this, a leap of faith is required if we are not to lapse into nihilist despair in the face of the meaningless of life or the fear of eternal damnation.

Commentary

The theme of this section is purification by fire. The dove, with its "flame of incandescent terror" (196), is a German plane bombing London, setting it on fire and killing thousands. But death is the only "discharge from sin and error" (198); only through dying to this world can we enter the next. Thus, the dove is also the Holy Spirit that at Pentecost descended to the Apostles as a tongue of fire when, after the crucifixion, Christ seemed to be dead. Our only freedom is the freedom to choose "pyre or pyre" (2000) – either to let the bombs kill us or to embrace faith in Christ while we are still living. Paradoxically (of course!), only through fire can humans be redeemed from despair – either the fires of war or the saving fire of Christ's grace. The present moment when war appears triumphant is as much a period of doubt about survival as that experienced by the Apostles, but the answer in both cases is faith. We either choose "hope, or else despair" (199) – the destructive or the redemptive fire.

It is, therefore, a valid question to ask who is responsible for devising "the torment" of sin and error that humanity endures (202). The answer is that it is the work of the agape Love of God. The "intolerable shirt of flame" (205) that London wears recalls the burning, poisoned shirt innocently given to Hercules by his wife, Deianeira. However, the shirt is just an image, and so is the German bombing. Even in peacetime, humanity suffers from a burning despair that "human power cannot remove" (206). Mankind must live through his trial and either be defeated by it or overcome it by the faith that the fires of hell can be overcome by the fires of religious fervor or Pentecost.

Summary of Part IV

The purifying fire of the Spirit redeems us from the devouring fire of sin through the death of our sinful bodies. We are not strong enough to evade the consequence of our sinful nature but God, who is Love, has the power to redeem us. He asks only that we come to Him in humility. The choice is ours. If we choose to cling to our selfish desires, we will be consumed by our sin. If we choose to seek Christ at the Still Point, God, who is Love, will redeem us with Pentecostal fire.

Part V Lines 209-234: "What we call the ... Calling."

Notes

"a step to the block, to the fire" (221) – Charles I was beheaded on Tuesday, January 30, 1649, outside the Banqueting House in Whitehall London. The German bombing campaign against the United Kingdom lasted from September 1940 to June 1941. Some 43,000 civilians were killed in London and other targeted cities. On May 10, 1941, alone, 3,000 Londoners died in Luftwaffe air raids.

Commentary

The section opens with the dominant motif of *Four Quartets*: beginnings and ends come together in the present moment. We begin some task because we have completed another task; when we come to the end of the new task, we shall begin another. Although the speaker does not yet draw this conclusion, the logic of this position is that death might will be a beginning. "The end is where we start from" (211).

The narrator speaks again of the struggle to express oneself in words – specifically to write poetry. Here, however, he is much more positive than when he wrote earlier in East Coker, "every attempt / Is a wholly new start, and a different kind of failure" (174-175). Each attempt to write is no longer seen as entirely new since it is now understood to be connected to the work that preceded it. Nor is failure seen as inevitable. In fact, success is celebrated, "every phrase / And sentence that is right [...] is an end and a beginning" (211-219). Everyone who has ever struggled to write will recognize that this is true because writing is not a collection of disconnected statements. Each statement is complete in itself but leads to the next. There are no breaks; writing is continuous, as is life.

The narrator spends time defining what makes a phrase or sentence "that is right" (212), and it all comes down to harmony – the individual words working together to form meaning so that "every word is at home, / Taking its place to support the others" (212-213). Some of the words are old, some new, some are common, and some formal, but there is no competition; there is only "The complete consort dancing together" (218). Such writing has the timeless quality of the dances described in *Burnt Norton* and *East Coker*. It is written in the moment, but it will outlive the moment. It will take its place in the pattern of tradition.

The Schmoop authors interpret this as a metaphor:

[T]he speaker's talking about *people* here, and the need for people to make the world into something beautiful by finding a sense of spiritual peace (or home) and supporting the people around them, too. Like the words in a sentence, people can't be too showy ("ostentatious"), but should find an easy way of bringing together what's traditional and what's modern ("An easy commerce of the old and new"). Further, people should seek out a way to express themselves plainly ("the common word exact") without falling into crudeness or "vulgarity." People should also be willing to speak in formal terms from time to time, but not in a jerky, self-absorbed way ("pedantic").

Although this is a perfectly reasonable extension or application of the speaker's words, I cannot see the metaphor. Earlier in *Four Quartets,* the narrator spoke at length about the difficulty of writing, and he seems to be revisiting the topic but with a more enlightened viewpoint.

Next, the narrator turns to consider mortality. He stresses that every action we begin is "a step to the block," recalling the execution of King Charles I; "to the fire," like London in flames each night; "down the sea's throat," like the fisherman in the waters off the Dry Salvages; "to an illegible stone," like the dead in the churchyard at Little Gidding (221-222). That is the knowledge we start with: we live and die with others who are dying, "we go with them" (224). Paradoxically, however, "We are born with the dead: / See, they return, and bring us with them" (225-226). The dead return in our memory, "The moment of the rose and the moment of the yew-tree / Are of equal duration" (227-228). Memory can make the past timeless by making it live in the present.

Having talked of individual experience, the narrator turns abruptly to generalize about an entire people. A people are trapped in linear time just like an individual, but just as memory can bring back a person so a nation's history can ensure that its people are "redeemed from time" (229). This is possible because "history is a pattern / Of timeless moments" (229-230). As we recall events from the past, we liberate them from the tyranny of duration. The idea here seems similar to that expressed in the poem "For the Fallen" (Sep. 1914) by Laurence Binyon (1869-1943):

> They shall grow not old, as we that are left grow old:
> Age shall not weary them, nor the years condemn.
> At the going down of the sun and in the morning
> We will remember them.

Schmoop also makes a connection with the message of Winston Churchill's famous speech of June 18, 1940, after the fall of France to the Germans:

> What General Weygand has called the Battle of France is over.
> I expect the Battle of Britain is about to begin. Upon this battle

depends the survival of Christian civilisation. Upon it depends our own British life, and the long continuity of our institutions and our Empire. The whole fury and might of the enemy must very soon be turned on us [… If] we fail, then the whole world, including the United States, including all that we have known and cared for, will sink into the abyss of a new dark age made more sinister, and perhaps more protracted, by the lights of perverted science. Let us therefore brace ourselves to our duties, and so bear ourselves that, if the British Empire and its Commonwealth last for a thousand years, men will still say, "This was their finest hour."

In recollecting the past of our history, we make that past timeless by bringing it alive in our present. That is what the narrator has been doing while in the "secluded chapel" of Little Gidding (231). He has been recalling those who lived and worshiped there and has returned them to the present. Thus, paradoxically, "while the light falls / On a winter's afternoon" (230-231), indicating the inevitable passage of time, "History is now and England" (232), indicating a dimension that transcends chronology.

Part V Lines 235-255: "We shall not cease … the rose are one."

Notes

"We shall not cease from…" (235) – It seems unlikely that Eliot was unaware of using the words from the hymn "Jerusalem":

> *I will not cease from* mental fight,
> Nor shall my sword sleep in my hand,
> Till we have built Jerusalem
> In England's green and pleasant land.

Whether consciously or not, Eliot may also be echoing the determination of Sir Winston Churchill in the darkest days of the war, "We shall not fail or falter; we shall not weaken or tire. We shall not fail or falter; we shall not weaken or tire." (BBC radio broadcast, Feb. 9, 1941).

"The unknown, remembered gate" (239) – *Burnt Norton*, "Through the first gate, / Into our first world" (20-21).

"the longest river" (242) – *The Dry Salvages*, "I think that the river / Is a strong brown god" (1-2). Americans like to claim the Mississippi as the world's longest river. Actually, it is the fourth-longest behind the Nile, the Amazon, and the Yangtze. It is, however, the longest river in North America.

"the children in the apple-tree" (244) – *Burnt Norton*, "There rises the hidden laughter / Of children in the foliage" (171-172).

"Between two waves of the sea" (247) – *The Dry Salvages*, "And the ragged rock in the restless waters, / Waves wash over it, fogs conceal it" (118-119).

137

"Quick now, here, now, always—" (248) – Compare *Burnt Norton*, "There rises the hidden laughter / Of children in the foliage / Quick now, here, always" (170-172).

"A condition of complete simplicity / (Costing no less that everything)" (249-250) – Compare Thoreau, "In proportion as [a man] simplifies his life, the laws of the universe will appear less complex" (*Walden* 18:8).

"the fire and the rose" (255) – The rose is a traditional symbol of love. Fire is the flame both of God's judgment and wrath and of the Spirit who purifies, warms, and enlightens.

Commentary

Confident in the love of God, man "shall not cease from exploration" (235). The end of our exploration is that we arrive back at where we started, but we have been changed by what we have experienced, and so it seems that we "know the place for the first time" (238). The narrator seems to be saying that we began with God and will return to God. He recalls descriptions of this state of returning earlier in the poem. In *Burnt Norton*, he encountered a gate he had never seen before, which reminded him of a gate in his past. This is expressed in the oxymoron, "the unknown, remembered gate" (239). This experience, coming near the end of his life, led him to a discovery about his earlier life, "When the last of earth left to discover / Is that which was the beginning" (240-241).

The source of "the longest river" (242) is the start of the narrator's life. He hears again, "The voice of the hidden waterfall / And the children in the apple-tree" (243-244). Those children were "Not known, because unlooked for" (245). So as a child, he never went to discover the identity of the children whose voices he heard. Perhaps he was just shy, but for whatever reason, they remained anonymous, and he never got to know them. Until now, the waterfall and the children had been forgotten, but now they come to mind. They are revealed in the moment of stillness, "Between two waves of the sea" (247).

The speaker repeats the message of the bird in *Burnt Norton*: focus intensely on the "now," the present, which is *here* and which is always the present. Complete simplicity and humility, placing oneself in the hands of God, is what we must attain. That is not easy since we will have to give up everything, like the rich man who asked Jesus, "Good Master, what good thing shall I do, that I may have eternal life?" to which Jesus replied, "If you want to be perfect, go, sell what you have, and give to the poor, and you will have treasure in heaven; and come, follow me" (*Matthew* 19:21, KJV). Yet if we can do this, then the fires of hell will be "in-folded / Into the crowned knot of fire / And the fire and the rose are one" (253-255). He seems to mean that we can live out the remainder of our lives with the spiritual conviction that God's love will resurrect us into eternal life.

Summary of Part V

Every birth is a beginning whose end will be death, which will lead to a new birth. The fleeting recovery of the rose in the garden of Burnt Norton is a timeless moment which, like the yew tree in the church yard, representing resurrection, redeems the times of death and transforms them into new patterns of life. We can only reach the Still Point in isolated moments within time and experience a momentary union with the divine. Complete union with the Still Point is the product of a lifetime's exploration. Achieving the simplicity and stillness of union with Christ costs everything. Yet all will be well when the purifying fire of the Spirit transforms us and reconciles us to God.

Four Quartets: *Burnt Norton, East Coker, The Dry Salvages, Little Gidding*

Reading Group Use of the Study Guide Questions

Although there are both closed and open questions in the Study Guide, very few of them have simple, right or wrong answers. They are designed to encourage in-depth discussion, disagreement, and (eventually) consensus. Above all, they aim to encourage readers to go to the text to support their conclusions and interpretations.

I am not so arrogant as to presume to tell readers how they should use this resource. I used it in the following ways, each of which ensured that group members were well prepared for group discussion and presentations.

1. Set a reading assignment for the group and tell everyone to be aware that the questions will be the focus of whole group discussion at the next meeting.

2. Set a reading assignment for the group and allocate particular questions to sections of the group (e.g. if there are four questions, divide the group into four sections, etc.).
In the meeting, form discussion groups containing one person who has prepared each question and allow time for feedback within the groups.
Have feedback to the whole the on each question by picking a group at random to present their answers and to follow up with a group discussion.

3. Set a reading assignment for the group, but do not allocate questions.
In the meeting, divide readers into groups and allocate to each group one of the questions related to the reading assignment, the answer to which they will have to present formally to the meeting.
Allow time for discussion and preparation.

4. Set a reading assignment for the group, but do not allocate questions.
In the meeting, divide readers into groups and allocate to each group one of the questions related to the reading assignment.
Allow time for discussion and preparation.
Now reconfigure the groups so that each group contains at least one person who has prepared each question and allow time for feedback within the groups.

5. Before starting to read the text, allocate specific questions to individuals or pairs. (It is best not to allocate all questions to allow for other approaches and variety. One in three questions or one in four seems about right.) Tell readers that they will be leading the group discussion on their question. They will need to start with a brief presentation of the issues and then conduct a question and answer session. After this, they will be expected to present a brief review of the discussion.

6. Having finished the text, arrange the meeting into groups of 3, 4 or 5. Tell each group to select as many questions from the Study Guide as there are members of the group.

Each individual is responsible for drafting out an answer to one question, and each answer should be substantial.

Each group as a whole is then responsible for discussing, editing and suggesting improvements to each answer.

Four Quartets: *Burnt Norton, East Coker,The Dry Salvages, Little Gidding*

Works Cited and Suggested Further Reading

I should add to the list below the Schmoop guide to the Four Quartets.

Anderson, Joel Edmund, "T.S. Eliot's 'Four Quartets.'" Resurrecting Orthodoxy. Jan. 2021. Web. Nov. 6, 2021.

Atkins, G. Douglas. *Reading T. S. Eliot: Four Quartets and the Journey Toward Understanding*. New York: Palgrave MacMillan, 2012.

Beauchamp, Scott, "Rediscovering Home," *Law and Liberty*. May 5, 2020. Web. Sep. 11, 2021.

Camus, Albert. The Myth of Sisyphus and Other Essays. Trans. Justin O'Brien. New York, Vintage Books, 1955.

Lachman, Gary. *Beyond the Robot: The Life and Work of Colin Wilson*. New York: TarcherPerigee, 2016.

Leiter, Deborah. TOWARD THE STILL POINT: T. S. ELIOT'S FOUR QUARTETS AND THOREAU'S WALDEN A Thesis Submitted to the College of Graduate Studies and Research in Partial Fulfillment of the Requirements for the Degree of Master of Arts in the Department of English University of Saskatchewan Saskatoon, Saskatchewan, Canada 2007

Longnecker, Dwight. "Listening to 'Burnt Norton.'" The Imaginative Conservative, Aug. 24, 2019. Web. Sep. 3, 2021.)

Mambrol, Nasrullah. "Analysis of T. S. Eliot's Four Quartets." Literary Theory and Criticism. July 4, 2020. Web. Nov. 7, 2021.

Matthiessen, F. O., *T. S. Eliot The Achievement of Poetry: An Essay on the Nature of Poetry*. New York: Galaxy, 1959.

Rajan, B. Ed. *T. S. Eliot A Study of his Writings by Several Hands*. New York: Haskell House, 1964.

Smidt, Kristian. *Poetry and Belief in the Work of T. S. Eliot*. Oslo: I Kommisjon Hos Jacob Dybwad, 1949.

Spender, Stephen. *T. S. Eliot*. New York: Viking Press, 1975.

Stanley, Colin. Ed. *The Ultimate Colin Wilson: Writings on Mysticism, Consciousness and Existentialism* London: Watkins, 2019.

Wilson, Colin. *The Angry Years: The Rise and Fall of the Angry Young Men*. London: Robson Books, 2007.

--- *Beyond the Occult*. London: Watkins, 2020.

---. *Super Consciousness: The Quest for the Peak Experience*. London: Watkins,

2019.

Worthen, John. *T. S. Eliot: A Short Biography*. London: Haus, 2009.

About the Author

Ray Moore was born in Nottingham, England. He obtained his Master's Degree in Literature from Lancaster University and taught in secondary education for twenty-eight years before relocating to Florida with his wife. There he taught English and Information Technology in the International Baccalaureate Program. He is now a full-time writer and fitness fanatic and leads a reading group at a local library.

Website: http://www.raymooreauthor.com

Ray strives to make his texts the best that they can be. If you have any comments or question about this book *please* contact the author through his email:

villageswriter@gmail.com

Also by Ray Moore:

Books are available as paperbacks and some from online eBook retailers.

Fiction:

1066: Year of the Five Kings is a novel of the most consequential year in the history of England.

The Darcys of Pemberley: A Sequel to 'Pride and Prejudice' by Jane Austen takes up the story of Elizabeth, Fitzwilliam, and Georgiana in the fateful year 1815.

The Reverend Lyle Thorne Mysteries

If you enjoy detective short stories, you will love my series featuring policeman turned vicar Lyle Thorne (1860-1947).

Investigations of The Reverend Lyle Thorne (Volume One)

Further Investigations of The Reverend Lyle Thorne (Volume Two)

Early Investigations of Lyle Thorne (Volume Three)

Sanditon Investigations of The Rev. Lyle Thorne (Volume Four)

Final Investigations of The Rev. Lyle Thorne (Volume Five)

Lost Investigation of The Rev. Lyle Thorne (Volume Six)

Official Investigations of Lyle Thorne (Volume Seven)

Clerical Investigations of The Rev. Lyle Thorne (Volume Eight)

More Clerical Investigations of The Rev. Lyle Thorne (Volume Nine)

Study Guide

Non-fiction:

Race and Education in America:

Slavery, The 1776 Report and American Education
Understanding the 1776 Report
Slavery, The 1619 Report and American Education (early 2022)
Understanding the 1619 Report (early 2022)

The **Critical Introduction series** is written for high school teachers and students and for college undergraduates. Each volume gives an in-depth analysis of a key text:

"The Stranger" by Albert Camus: A Critical Introduction (Revised Second Edition)
"The General Prologue" by Geoffrey Chaucer: A Critical Introduction
"Pride and Prejudice" by Jane Austen: A Critical Introduction
"The Great Gatsby" by F. Scott Fitzgerald: A Critical Introduction

The **Text and Critical Introduction series** differs from the Critical introduction series as these books contain the original text and in the case of the medieval texts an interlinear translation to aid the understanding of the text. The commentary allows the reader to develop a deeper understanding of the text and themes within the text.

"Sir Gawain and the Green Knight": Text and Critical Introduction*
"The General Prologue" by Geoffrey Chaucer: Text and Critical Introduction*
"Heart of Darkness" by Joseph Conrad: Text and Critical Introduction*
"Henry V" by William Shakespeare: Text and Critical Introduction*
"Oedipus Rex" by Sophocles: Text and Critical Introduction*
"A Room with a View" By E.M. Forster: Text and Critical Introduction*
"The Sign of Four" by Sir Arthur Conan Doyle Text and Critical Introduction
"The Wife of Bath's Prologue and Tale" by Geoffrey Chaucer: Text and Critical Introduction*
Jane Austen: The Complete Juvenilia: Text and Critical Introduction
Jane Austen: Lady Susan, The Watsons, Sanditon: Text and Critical Introduction

Study Guides - listed alphabetically by author

Study Guides offer an in-depth look at aspects of a text. They generally include an introduction to the characters, genre, themes, setting, tone of a text. They also may include activities on helpful literary terms as well as graphic organizers to aid understanding of the plot and different perspectives of characters.

Some guides include the text which is reflected in the Title as *Study Guide with Text to…*.

* indicates only available as an eBook

Study Guide to "ME and EARL and the Dying GIRL" by Jesse Andrews

Study Guide to "Alias Grace" by Margaret Atwood

Study Guide to "The Handmaid's Tale" by Margaret Atwood

Study Guide to "The Testaments" by Margaret Atwood

Study Guide to "Pride and Prejudice" by Jane Austen

Study Guide to "Moloka'i" by Alan Brennert

Study Guide on "Jane Eyre" by Charlotte Brontë

Study Guide to "Wuthering Heights" by Emily Brontë

Study Guide to "The Myth of Sisyphus" by Albert Camus

Study Guide to "The Stranger" by Albert Camus

Study Guides to "The Myth of Sisyphus" and "The Stranger" by Albert Camus

Study Guide to "Death Comes to the Archbishop" by Willa Cather

Study Guide to Seven Short Stories by Kate Chopin

Study Guide to "The Awakening" by Kate Chopin

Study Guide to "Ready Player One" by Ernest Cline

Study Guide to "The Water Dancer" by Ta-Nehisi Coates

Study Guide to "Disgrace" by J. M. Coetzee

Study Guide to "Heart of Darkness" by Joseph Conrad*

Study Guide to "The Meursault Investigation" by Kamel Daoud

Study Guide on "Great Expectations" by Charles Dickens

Study Guide to "The Sign of Four" by Sir Arthur Conan Doyle.

Study Guide to Six Classic Sherlock Holmes Stories by Sir Arthur Conan Doyle

Study Guide with Text to Six Classic Sherlock Holmes Stories by Sir Arthur Conan Doyle

Study Guide to "Manhattan Beach" by Jennifer Egan

Study Guide to "The Mill on the Floss" by George Eliot*

Study Guide

Study Guide to "The Wasteland, Prufrock and Poems" by T.S. Eliot

Study Guide to "Medea" by Euripides

Study Guide with Text to "Medea" by Euripides

Study Guide on "Birdsong" by Sebastian Faulks

Study Guide to "The Great Gatsby" by F. Scott Fitzgerald

Study Guide to "A Room with a View" by E. M. Forster

Study Guide with Text to "Selected Poems" by Robert Frost (1913-1923)

Study Guide to "Lord of the Flies" by William Golding

Study Guide to "Looking for Alaska" by John Green

Study Guide to "Paper Towns" by John Green

Study Guide to "Turtles All the Way Down" by John Green

Study Guide to "Florida" by Lauren Groff

Study Guide on "Catch-22" by Joseph Heller

Study Guide to "Unbroken" by Laura Hillenbrand

Study Guide to "A Thousand Splendid Suns" by Khaled Hosseini

Study Guide to "The Kite Runner" by Khaled Hosseini

Study Guide to "A Shropshire Lad" by A. E. Housman

Study Guide with Text to "A Shropshire Lad" by A. E. Housman

Study Guide with Text to "Last Poems" by A. E. Housman

Study Guide with Text to "More Poems" and "Additional Poems" by A. E. Housman

Study Guide to "On the Road" by Jack Kerouac

Study Guide to "The Secret Life of Bees" by Sue Monk Kidd

Study Guide on "The Invention of Wings" by Sue Monk Kidd

Study Guide to "Fear and Trembling" by Søren Kierkegaard

Study Guide to "Go Set a Watchman" by Harper Lee

Study Guide to "Pachinko" by Min Jin Lee

Study Guide on "Life of Pi" by Yann Martel

Study Guide to "Death of a Salesman" by Arthur Miller

Study Guide to "The Bluest Eye" by Toni Morrison

Study Guide to "Reading Lolita in Tehran" by Azir Nafisi

Study Guide to "The Sympathizer" by Viet Thanh Nguyen

Study Guide to "Animal Farm" by George Orwell

Study Guide on "Nineteen Eighty-Four" by George Orwell

148

New titles are added regularly.

Readers' Guides – only available as eBooks

Readers' Guides offer an introduction to important aspects of the text and questions for personal reflection and/or discussion. Guides are written for individual readers who wish to explore texts in depth and for members of Reading Circles who wish to make their discussions of texts more productive.

A Reader's Guide to Becoming by Michelle Obama
A Reader's Guide to Educated: A Memoir by Tara Westover

Teacher resources: Ray also publishes many more study guides and other resources for classroom use on the 'Teachers Pay Teachers' website:
http://www.teacherspayteachers.com/Store/Raymond-Moore